Thriveology

Thriveology

Resilience-Informed Teaching
through the CARING Model

HEEKAP LEE

Foreword by Rhoda C. Sommers

WIPF & STOCK · Eugene, Oregon

THRIVEOLOGY
Resilience-Informed Teaching through the CARING Model

Wipf & Stock
An Imprint of Wipf and Stock Publishers
199 W. 8th Ave., Suite 3
Eugene, OR 97401

www.wipfandstock.com

PAPERBACK ISBN: 978-1-7252-9466-0
HARDCOVER ISBN: 978-1-7252-9467-7
EBOOK ISBN: 978-1-7252-9468-4

OCTOBER 11, 2021

Contents

List of Figures and Tables

FIGURES

TABLES

Foreword

As a long-time educational psychology instructor and teacher education professor, looking at Jesus as the master teacher and learning from his interactions with students has been one of my passions. Teacher education students from three different Christian universities in the United States have explored this topic with me in the courses I taught. In addition, I asked teachers in China and India to study Jesus as the master teacher with me, and I gained much insight through their thoughts and perspectives, which were so different than mine. For my students and me, these conversations have shaped our teaching and permanently altered our perspective of Jesus as a teacher. His relational, student-centered, prepared-yet-flexible, and goal-oriented approach holds much for all who teach and influence others. The book Dr. HeeKap Lee has written augments the learning experiences of my students and me.

I have been privileged to work with many incredible colleagues who have impacted my life, thoughts, and beliefs during these past twenty-two years in higher education. One of the finest of these colleagues is Dr. Lee. We first met in 2006 when both of us were involved in teacher education work at a Christian university in the Midwest. I was drawn to his thoughtfulness, perseverance, and positive perspective in spite of life's disappointment, pain, and trauma. Dr. Lee's heart is one of love and shalom. He desires deeply that the teacher education students who pass through his classroom are well prepared to not only teach effectively but to also reflect dispositions needed to positively impact the students in their classrooms. Jesus, as the master teacher, is the model Dr. Lee has for himself as well as for his students.

Dr. Lee wrote this book during the COVID-19 pandemic. Though we are seeing hope for the ending of the pandemic, there is still much uncertainty, spread of the virus, and ongoing trauma. Our world remains upended and unsettled. What education will look like moving forward remains unpredictable. In the pandemic, P–12 education suffered greatly as have its teachers. It will most likely be years before many students regain the learning that has been disrupted and the trauma and loss that has been experienced will follow them for a lifetime. Teachers have faced incredible pressure and stress as they have done all they could to help students learn. Their trauma is no less real than what their students have and are experiencing. While P–12 teachers have always had long-lasting influence in their students' lives, the challenges they face are even greater as we look to the future. Both the teachers and students need knowledge, skills, and dispositions to guide them through the current crisis as well as face a variable and unknowable future.

In *Thriveology*, Dr. Lee develops and uses the CARING model as a way for teachers to help their students deal with trauma and not only become resilient, but thrive. The six elements of the CARING model include Cultivating connections, Affirming personhood, restoring relationships, Initiating inquiry, Nurturing socioemotional learning, and Gaining community actualization. This model is explored and illustrated through Jesus' interactions and teaching of his students who were traumatized. Each chapter is replete with practical teaching and relational advice for teachers as well as glimpses of Dr. Lee's heart of love and shalom for all students.

This book speaks to my heart as a teacher and leader and encourages me to focus on relationships, to lead and teach with inquiry, and to engage in community actualization. Traditional American culture is individualistic, which is reflected in Maslow's hierarchy of self-actualization as the ultimate goal; however, Dr. Lee's emphasis on community actualization is a biblical ideal. Jesus made the ultimate sacrifice so we could live in community and thrive in spite of the pain and trauma of life. No one is able to truly thrive without community.

In many ways, Dr. Lee has exposed his heart and soul through *Thriveology*. In each page I hear his life of commitment to Jesus, love for others, humility, and quest for pedagogy that reflects these beliefs. This quest has been central in his profession and research. I liken his use of the Beatitudes and case studies of Jesus' teaching to rereading favorite stories with new eyes. This satisfies both my spiritual and professional drives. I am convinced you will have the same experience.

September 2021
Rhoda C. Sommers, Ph.D.
Dean of Health, Human and Public Services,
Clark State College

Preface

THREE YEARS AGO, I took a sabbatical to research the topic of "thriveology." Since that moment, I am convinced that the purpose of education is to make all students thrive, not merely survive, no matter what situations and contexts students experience. I believe the purpose of education is fulfilled when our God-given talents and gifts are fully identified, developed, and utilized to build the community of shalom. Therefore, the pedagogy of thriveology starts by recognizing each student as the image-bearer of God, who equipped all with gifts and abilities. The next task is developing students effectively by providing quality instructions as well as relevant interventions to promote their attitudes and disposition through which students continue to build future communities of shalom. However, the American education system does not encourage our students to thrive because of three dominating approaches and ideologies.

First, American education has adopted a reductionist approach ever since the introduction of behaviorism. Behaviorism asks us to analyze students' behaviors and learning contents in manageable and observable small parts. All learning tasks are chopped into narrowly identified facts and arranged systematically. A teacher is to feed spoonful pieces of information to students so that students can digest concepts without confusion or discomfort. Challenging students with triggering tasks and using creative disequilibrium strategies are discouraged. This paradigm renders students as babies who need to be cradled by providing a much too comfortable classroom environment.

Second, American education has been dominated by Procrustean-bed philosophy. Teachers create the learning objectives along with the class norms and routines by drawing a line between normal (standard) and abnormal (deviant). Students are highly monitored based on this kind of a dichotomist rule, and punishments are applied severely for the abnormal.

The success of education is to assimilate abnormal students (students who have different learning needs, such as ELs, special education students, minority, disadvantaged students, etc.) into American mainstream culture and its attending values and norms. Many scholars argue that the American education system kills students' creativity.

Lastly, a positivistic trend has ruled American education. This marks the strong influence of capitalism on education, encouraging success to be verified by tangible proof and quantifiable evidence. The success of education is justified with increased numbers, such as test scores, number of college acceptances, GPA scores, etc. Education is focused only on visible and observable areas, ignoring developments in non-cognitive, social-emotional, and spiritual dimensions. Students are pressured to outperform their peers in academic areas, considering their classmates as competitors rather than companions because only a few advance. Classrooms are turning into battlefields.

I am writing this book in the midst of the COVID-19 pandemic. We have encountered a new era that gives us unprecedented ways of thinking regarding educational programs and interventions. In fact, the COVID-19 pandemic gives us new insights into American education, allowing us to change its trajectory through the pedagogy of thriveology. The COVID-19 pandemic has taught us to transform education for students in order to fit new definitions of thriving. The traditional mode of education no longer works for students to thrive in our turbulent, drastically changing society. That's why I recommend us to take on a new educational approach, changing our focus from competition-oriented to collaboration-centered; from individual student success to thriving in community together; from focusing on developing cognitive, visible areas to social-emotional, non-cognitive dimensions; from narrowly divided content to holistic curriculum; from measuring quantitative change to measuring the well-being of humans in community. In order to implement the theory of thriveology, I suggest a framework for teachers to implement in their classrooms, called CARING. CARING is an acronym for the six stages that teachers may take in their classroom teaching: 1) Cultivating connections, 2) Affirming personhoods, 3) Restoring relationships, 4) Initiating inquiry, 5) Nurturing SEL, and 6) Gaining community actualization.

This book consists of three sections. In the first (chapters 1 and 2), I explain basic concepts and the foundational theories of resilience-informed teaching, along with an introduction of the CARING model. The second section (chapters 3–10) identifies eight different cases where students experience trauma with relevant teaching interventions based on the CARING model. Lastly (chapters 11–12), I culminate a resilience-informed lesson based on the teaching of Jesus, who teaches his disciples who experience trauma in Mark 6. I also show a lesson plan to teach traumatized students effectively. Finally, I introduce the GREAT competency model, identifying key competencies and dispositions of an effective teacher.

Many people have unanimously pointed to the difficulty of teaching students while in a pandemic; however, I believe the power of education is for teachers to ensure that students thrive no matter the situation. Effective teachers always leave their legacy through their teaching in and out of the classroom. I hope this book will be used to strengthen their beliefs and competencies.

HeeKap Lee
September 2021

Acknowledgements

THERE ARE MANY WHO have contributed in no small measure to the success of this book project. First of all, I thank Azusa Pacific University (APU), which allowed me to conduct my initial research on thriveology three years ago by offering me sabbatical research leave. This sabbatical time uncovered opportunities to continue pursuing research as I currently research with my colleagues in support groups on a monthly basis. This book project is supported by APU's Publication Assistance Grant.

I want to share my special thanks to my two colleagues at Azusa Pacific University, Dr. Calvin Roso and Dr. Janet Hansen, who read through the first manuscript iteration and provided constructive feedback and comments. In addition, I thank my daughter, Sharon Lee, an LAUSD high school English teacher, who provided feedback based on her teaching experiences. My family, my wife (Yun Sim) and son (Isaac), have never ceased to support me with their encouragement and prayers during this past year of book drafting. Finally, I thank God, who gave me the strength with his wisdom and knowledge to complete this book project.

HeeKap Lee

1

Thriveology and Teaching Resilience

Take heart! I have overcome the world

(JOHN 16:33)

INTRODUCTION

EVEN WITH A PLETHORA of educational reforms, American schools still experience many issues, including high rates of substance abuse, violence, crime, bullying, teen pregnancy, and suicide among youth.[1] In addition, since COVID-19 has surged globally, schools have shut down and students have struggled with academic as well as social and emotional trauma. These experienced chronic traumas and adversities continually result in mental, physical, cognitive, social, and spiritual developmental disorders among students.[2]

Can our students learn something positive for themselves in spite of painful and challenging school contexts? Can our students thrive in their cognitive, emotional, and social dimensions to transform their toxic

---

1. See works such as Garbarino, "Educating Children"; Peterson and Deal, "How Leaders Influence"; Jenson, *Brain-Based Learning*; Gruenert and Whitaker, *School Culture Rewired*; Park, "Building Strengths of Character"; Woolfolk, *Educational Psychology*.

2. See Hoare, "Toxic Effect"; Garbarino, "Educating Children"; Jensen, *Brain-Based Learning*.

environments? If so, what do teachers need to do to implement thriveology for students in and out of the classroom? Which kind of strategies should be emphasized?

The term *thriving* is defined as a set of dispositional characteristics that promote positive outcomes even under toxic educational environments. It leads to students' academic as well as social success in three areas: academic engagement and performance, interpersonal relationships, and psychological well-being.[3] How can teachers promote thriving for students? Researchers agree that thriving depends on contending with the vigorous struggles of pain and challenge in students' lives. When students experience difficulties, they are given the opportunity to learn and experience happiness more deeply and enjoy hard-earned rewards as well as physical well-being, academic success, care for others, and commitment to a healthy lifestyle.[4] There are several ways to help students thrive through difficulties and challenges, including allowing setbacks, embracing challenges positively, and developing a growth mindset.[5]

This chapter will share some education strategies on how to provide an atmosphere where students can thrive while experiencing trauma and challenges along with applicable interventions for teachers to utilize in their classrooms.

FROM SURVIVING TO THRIVING

There are four possible responses and consequences when people experience physical, psychological, emotional, relational, and spiritual adversity.[6] The first option would be succumbing, in which traumatized people continue to downslide and finally are extinguished. Survival would be the second option, where traumatized people may survive, but their outcome is weaker and unproductive. The third option, recovery, is a return to the pre-adversity level of functioning, a return that can be either rapid or more gradual. The final response, which is the main theme of this book, is thriving. Traumatized people surpass their adverse events in some manner. The figure below is the summary of four possible responses.

3. Schreiner, "Thriving," 12.
4. Benson, "On a Path toward Thriving"; Pearsall, *Beethoven Factor*.
5. Simeon, "Got Grit?"
6. Carver, "Resilience and Thriving"; O'Leary and Ickovics, "Resilience and Thriving."

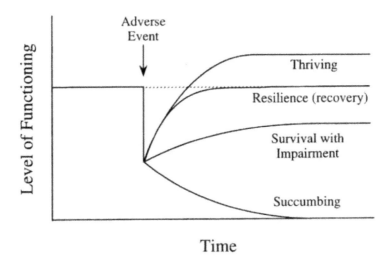

Figure 1.1: **Four Responses to Trauma**[7]

Succumbing

When a person experiences trauma, it negatively affects his/her performance until the individual succumbs.

Survival

Trauma seriously affects the human brain and body. When children are exposed to complex or acute trauma, the brain shifts its operation from development to stress response.[8] When brains are triggered by trauma, they release chemicals into the body to allow us to survive those states of distress. When we sense we are in danger, the brain switches to survival mode: fight (acting out), flight (withdrawing), or freeze (going numb) responses in action. In survival mode, the learning environment can suffer and tremendously stressed brains can't teach/learn.[9]

---

7. This figure is adopted from Carver, "Resilience and Thriving," 246.
8. Souers and Hall, *Fostering Resilient Learners*, 21.
9. Sours and Hall, *Fostering Resilient Learners*, 29.

When a student is exposed to a traumatic event, it triggers the natural fight-or-flight response. If the student remains in that fight-or-flight mode, physiological changes can occur, including inhibited brain and physical development. Surviving simply means to continue to live or exist. When uncertain and unexpected events happen, students respond in a way that enables them to keep on existing. Their quality of life, however, has been diminished because they are unable to adapt to unexpected events. The table below is the summary of the three features of survival mode[10].

Table 1.1: Three Features of Survival Mode

Flight	Fight	Freezing
withdrawing, fleeing and skipping class; daydreaming; seeming to sleep; avoiding other students; hiding from others; wandering; becoming disengaged;	acting out; being silly; behaving aggressively; exhibiting defiance; being hyperactive; arguing, screaming, and yelling;	exhibiting numbness; refusing to answer; refusing to get needs met; giving a blank look; feeling unable to move or act;

How do we respond to students in survival mode? A twofold intervention is effective: individual connection to each student and creating a supportive learning environment. For personal connections, talking about the issue with the student and teaching students the importance of self-care is critical. Furthermore, creating a consistent and predictable classroom environment is another critical strategy for teachers to consider. Wright[11] suggests the following interventions:

- Discuss, rehearse, and frequently revisit rules, expectations and rewards;

- Avoid threats, intimidation, and battles for control;

- Reinforce that schools are a nonviolent and safe place for children, both physically and emotionally;

- Integrate safety and conflict resolution skills throughout the curriculum;

10. Souers and Hall, *Fostering Resilient Learners*, 29.

11. Wright, "Truth, but Not Yet," 148–49.

- Emphasize causal and sequential relationships in classroom activities;

- Divide tasks and instruction into parts to help students feel less overwhelmed;

- Provide concrete examples and use visual cues, physical movement, and recall activities during instruction to help children stay focused and engaged; and

- Offer ongoing support and encouragement to support staying on task.

Recovery

Recovery refers to the ability to bounce back from adversity, frustration, and misfortune to the pre-traumatic status.[12] It is not making problems go away, but gives students the ability to see their life patterns in the past, find enjoyment in life, and better handle stress.[13] There are two main interventions for students who experience trauma and adversity: 1) focusing on promoting students' dispositions and non-cognitive skills; and 2) supporting social relationships among students.

Character development, mindfulness training, relaxation techniques, regular exercise, and stress-coping strategies are effective interventions to promote students' resilience. There are six psychosocial factors that promote resilience in individuals: 1) optimism, 2) cognitive flexibility, 3) active coping skills, 4) maintaining a supportive social network, 5) attending to one's physical well-being, and 6) embracing a personal moral compass.[14] Secondly, helping students see these qualities as an integral part of the school community through collaborative activities is another effective intervention.[15]

Thriving

The concept of thriving refers to a person's ability to go beyond their original level of functioning and to grow and function despite repeated exposure to

---

12. Ledesma, "Conceptual Frameworks," 1.
13. Honsinger and Brown, "Preparing Trauma-Sensitive Teachers."
14. Nugent et al., "Resilience after Trauma."
15. Conn et al., "Creating a Culture of Care."

stressful and traumatic environments.[16] Thriving is a condition beyond re-silience and surviving, when reinvention occurs after an uncertain or unex-pected event. Research shows that students learn more actively when they confront trauma and adversities and difficult situations.[17] Bandura[18] posits that "when faced with obstacles, setbacks, and failures, those who have strong belief in their capabilities redouble their effort to master challenges."

Thriving can be fulfilled through two ways.[19] First, thriving occurs when people are able to successfully cope with adversities and difficulties in their lives, through which they learn and grow. Second, people thrive when they relate with each other, nurturing others to seize life opportunities for growth so that they also challenge adversity as a mechanism for positive growth and development. Eventually, all people can build a safe and coop-erative community together, instilling a positive organizational culture that provides a safe, supportive, encouraging, and challenging environment.

THREE DIMENSIONS OF THRIVING

Thriving should be the foundational method of teaching in a time like this. As I write this book, students are struggling with serious academic and so-cial/emotional traumas due to COVID-19. However, the goal of education is to thrive, where students reach their full potential—academically, social-ly, and spiritually—in the face of adversity. The mechanism to ensure this transformation is through the prospect of resilience-informed teaching,[20] consisting of six components of teaching (the CARING model).

In this section, I will explain the term *thriving* in depth. What does the term *thriving* mean? Student thriving can be accomplished in three di-mensions: personal, relational, and cultural thriving. First, students need to develop non-cognitive skills through which they are willing to leave their comfort zone to redefine adversity as an essential source from which to

---

16. Ledesma, "Conceptual Frameworks," 1.

17. Several other studies point to this same conclusion. See Peasall, *Beethoven Effect*; Dweck, *Mindset*.

18. Bandura, "Social Cognitive Theory," 120.

19. Feeney and Collins, "Thriving through Relationships."

20. I believe that the purpose of education is to thrive. Students who experience trauma and adversity need to fulfill personal, relational, as well as cultural thriving in and out of classrooms. In order to thrive, I recommend teachers to implement resilience-informed teaching, through the CARING model introduced in this book.

grow and lead positive change. Second, students assist and challenge others to reframe adversity as well. Cultural thriving is the last dimension of the pedagogy of thriveology. The goal is to build a school environment where students are fully encouraged and motivated to learn by creating a cooperative school culture. The figure below depicts the summary of the three dimensions of the pedagogy of thriveology.

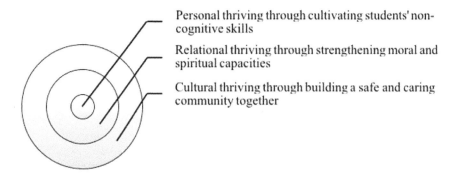

Personal thriving through cultivating students' non-cognitive skills

Relational thriving through strengthening moral and spiritual capacities

Cultural thriving through building a safe and caring community together

Figure 1.2: Three Dimensions of the Pedagogy of Thriveology

Personal Thriving: Cultivating Students' Non-Cognitive Skills

As mentioned in the previous section of this chapter, researchers have recognized a specific capacity that contributes to student success, known alternately as "grit," "growth mindset," "perseverance," "resilience," and "curiosity." However, many researchers have argued that there are many non-cognitive factors and skills that contribute to students' academic as well as career success. The term "non-cognitive skill" refers to attributes and interpersonal resources that lead more directly to students' academic as well as career success. Non-cognitive skills influence a student's school performance as well as reach into their adulthood. Studies across the fields of education, economics, and psychology indicate that non-cognitive skills predict a variety of adult outcomes, including academic achievement, employment, financial stability, criminal behavior, and health.[21]

How do we define non-cognitive skills? Hoerr presents them as five success skills: empathy, self-control, integrity, embracing diversity, and

---

21. Gabrieli et al., *Ready to Be Counted*.

grit.[22] Luthans, Youssef, and Avolio classify four categories of psychological capitals, including self-efficacy, hope, optimism, and resilience.[23] McMillan summarizes twelve factors including attitude, interests, values, self-monitoring, integrity, self-efficacy, self-esteem, interpersonal relationship, altruism, and perseverance.[24] One comprehensive model of non-cognitive factors was hypothesized by Farrington and colleagues[25] at the University of Chicago Consortium on Chicago School Research (CCSR), which includes five non-cognitive factors: academic mindset, academic perseverance, academic behavior, social skills, and learning strategies. The table below depicts a summary of these five non-cognitive skills.

Table 1.2: Non-Cognitive Skills

Non-Cognitive Skills	Descriptions
Academic behaviors	Student actions related to attending class, participating in class discussions, completing assignments
Academic perseverance	Student ability to remain focused and engaged in work despite distractions, setbacks or obstacles
Social skills	Interpersonal qualities such as cooperation, assertion, responsibility, and empathy
Learning strategies	Students' ability to self-regulate, set goals, employ study skills
Academic mindset	Students' beliefs, attitudes or ways of perceiving oneself in relation to learning

How can students cultivate these non-cognitive skills? The key would be to improve students' self-efficacy in and out of the classroom. In order to do that, three applicable practices have been suggested. First, teachers may cultivate students' non-cognitive skills in the classroom by helping them to notice positive experiences, making classroom activities enjoyable. Strategies include telling resilient stories and fostering flow while students

22. Hoerr, *Formative Five.*

23. Luthans et al., *Psychological Capital.*

24. McMillian, *Classroom Assessment.*

25. Farrington et al., *Role of Noncognitive Factors.*

are engaged in challenging learning tasks. Second, students' usage of their challenges and failing experiences as opportunities is critical. For example, when students experience setbacks and overcome them, they learn that if they try again and harder they can succeed. Teachers may encourage students to take a step outside of their comfort zone and take on a challenge where the outcome is not guaranteed. Pearsall[26] discovered the value of the stress-induced growth concept, where students' suffering refreshed their memory about the importance of looking for inspiration from those who learned to thrive through crisis.

Third, using engagement strategies encourage students' growth in non-cognitive capacities. For example, Bashant[27] suggests strategies such as turning the problem into a picture or puzzle, starting with the why before the what, encouraging students to work in communities, and rewarding hard work. In addition, initiating a discussion about adversity, encouraging students to learn about people who overcome adversity, and developing students' long-term goals are effective strategies.

In the CARING model, personal thriving will be accomplished through their social and emotional competencies and skills. Social emotional learning focuses on five emotional skills, including self-awareness, self-management, social awareness, relationship skills, and responsible decision-making.[28] We will learn more about this matter throughout this book.

Relational Thriving: Strengthening Students' Social-Relational Capacities

The second dimension of the pedagogy of thriveology is to strengthen students' social, relational capacities. When they are equipped with non-cognitive skills, they gain insight to redefine adversity as a mechanism for positive change. Then, they help other students who may experience difficulty and challenge by positively relating with them. Spiritual and moral capacities are necessary to relate with others in and out of the classroom because classrooms are spiritual spaces.

Education is a meaning-making process through which students gain knowledge of themselves in relationship to other people and outside

26. Pearsall, *Beethoven Effect*.
27. Bashant, "Developing Grit."
28. Collaborative for Academic, Social, and Emotional Learning (CASEL).

realities. Education helps students highlight their ultimate concern and focuses their core values around a central philosophy of life, whether religious or not. Hence, the teacher's responsibility in education is to inspire absolute respect for human dignity as well as a sense of universal worth to learners.

Benson, Roehlkepartain, and Rude[29] view spirituality as an important dimension of human development that is closely linked to an individual's personal and social well-being. Nord[30] concludes that the major reason for school violence lies in the spiritual emptiness or spiritual darkness found in students. Nodding[31] recommends that the only way to improve is to introduce the loving and encouraging spirits of teachers into school. I believe that the future depends on caring enough to invest time and money to help engage our students. Palmer[32] affirms that spirituality helps students make the best use of these values for self-growth and provides benefits to others and society at large.

Research has found many positive results for improving students' spirituality. For example, students who score high on measures of spirituality are less likely than their peers to engage in violence or other antisocial behavior.[33] In addition, they were more likely to cope with crisis situations by being hopeful and proactive and not engaging in self-destructive behavior.[34]

How can we cultivate students' moral and spiritual capacities in the classroom? First, spiritual competencies such as honesty, respect, and caring among students should be embedded and incorporated into the curriculum. Kagan suggests teaching students caring, respect, and common virtue, addressing "the breakdown of community and morality among students by making character education a part of the school's core curriculum."[35]

Second, students' moral and ethical capacities can be enhanced through a certain learning process or task. For example, Nord[36] identifies four learning processes through which students can cultivate spirituality. Those processes are dialogue, practice, confirmation, and modeling.

29. Benson et al., "Spiritual Development in Childhood."

30. Nord, *Religion and American Education.*

31. Nodding, *Caring.*

32. Palmer, *Courage to Teach.*

33. See Windham et al., "Selected Factors."

34. See Elkins et al., "Toward a Humanistic-Phonological Spirituality."

35. Kagan, "Teaching for Character," 51.

36. Nord, *Religion and American Education.*

Gersch[37] suggests that spiritual listening allows for students to be motivated by their personal drives and meanings. Closely listening to students on a deep level means that students attach their longings, purposes, and activities to their lives. Beechick[38] also identifies a set of spiritual development tasks that students need to develop, which includes continuing to develop healthy relationships with others.

Thirdly, Zohar and Marshall[39] outline some useful competencies, skills, or qualities of a spiritually intelligent person. They identify key components of spiritual intelligence, such as a higher degree of self-awareness, the capacity to be inspired by vision and values, the ability to face and use suffering and transcend pain, a holistic worldview, an appreciation of diversity, being field independent, spontaneity, a marked tendency to ask why or what questions and seek fundamental answers, and compassion.

Relational thriving competencies will be accomplished throughout the CARING processes, specifically emphasized in the CARING stages of cultivating connections and restoring relationships, which will be explained in the next chapter.

Cultural Thriving: Cultivating a Positive and Cooperative School Culture

The last dimension of the pedagogy of thriveology is to cultivate a positive and cooperative school culture. This is a cooperative endeavor where all stakeholders work together to build a safe educational community. Many educators worry about toxic school cultures, easily identified with the following characteristics: no clear purpose, hostile relationships among stakeholders, an absence of honest dialogue. Mayer[40] enumerated the variables of school that promote students' antisocial behavior: an over-reliance on punitive methods of control, unclear rules for student deportment, lack of student involvement, and lack of understanding student differences.

There are two ways of change: change from the outside in and change from the inside out. However, most school renovation approaches tend to highlight the external structure, the means, rather than the internal changes sought, such as encouraging students to be better equipped for the current

37. Gersch, "Positive Future."
38. Beechick, *Biblical Psychology of Learning.*
39. Zohar and Marshall, *Spiritual Intelligence.*
40. Mayer, "Behavioral Strategies," 85.

age in terms of knowledge, skill, socialization, and character. A better way to address this might be to focus on internal changes and to make the delivery method secondary. The most important factor is the school community itself, where the school should commit to the implemented innovation.

How can educators and school leaders cooperatively work together to build a school as a safe place and better education agent? Langer, Hall, and McMartin[41] identify three factors that work closely in order to implement an educational initiative: 1) the context of a community that demonstrates a shared vision for flourishing life, 2) involvement of all aspects of the person in the given education program, and 3) the modeling of individuals who demonstrate the intervention. In order to build a positive learning culture within a school, the school as a whole should align with the new direction and goal of education within the school. Three suggestions follow regarding this implementation.

First, change in the school should be initiated by inserting a growth mindset to cultivate students' non-cognitive skills. A growth mindset correlates with openness to new learning and a belief in the teachers' ability to help all students grow and learn. Having a growth mindset culture may contribute to factors supporting the development of culturally responsive teaching, culturally responsive organizational learning, and increased multicultural organizational efficacy, resulting in improved school outcomes.[42] In order to cultivate students' non-cognitive skills and moral, spiritual capacities, the school also needs to develop corresponding skills throughout the school so that all school systems act as a single entity with its own goals, values, and organizational behaviors. Growth mindset interventions include sharing information with faculty so that they can change and grow through learning and effort. Bandura[43] explains that the well-being of the individual students within a school depends on the alignment of the individuals' goals with the system's goals.

Second, creating a positive and cooperative school culture should be the direction of school change. What does "positive and cooperative" mean? It means that the school should be a place of collaboration, mutual respect, communication, kindness, and encouragement.[44] The school should be a place of welcome and care by providing a social support mechanism

41. Langer, *Power of Mindful Learning*.

42. See Dweck, "Mindsets and Human Nature"; Walton, "New Science."

43. Bandura, "Social Cognitive Theory."

44. Peterson and Deal, *Shaping School Culture*.

to allow for the meaningful participation of all stakeholders. Changes in school climate were shown to leverage improvements in school outcomes. These school changes include individual agency, collaborative decision-making, recognition of the individual nature of meaning-making, openness to change, and psychosocial support including mindset interventions.

Finally, schools must operate at a systemic viewpoint. For example, Hoy et al.[45] identify three factors that cultivate school effectiveness: academic emphasis, collective efficacy, and trust. Academic emphasis can be achieved by setting realistic academic goals for students, and by providing an orderly and serious learning environment where students are motivated to work hard and respect academic achievement. Collective efficacy is another key factor for effective schooling as teachers will together organize and execute the course of action required to have a positive effect on students.[46] Trust among faculty, parents, and students is the last factor. Trust refers to "a willingness to be vulnerable to another party based on the confidence that that party is benevolent, reliable, competent, honest and open."[47] Trust among teachers, parents, and students produced schools that showed marked gains in student learning, whereas schools with weak trust relationships saw virtually no improvement. Pepler[48] asserts that all school teachers and leaders have the crucial role of social architect to ensure that students' social lives are structured to encourage the development of healthy and egalitarian social relationships.

Emphasizing cultural thriving is a unique feature of the CARING model. The focus of resilience-informed teaching is not on each student's academic success or well-being, but rather on gaining community actualization.

CONCLUDING REMARKS

Jesus says that we will experience trouble and trauma while living in this world. He told his disciples in John 16:33: "I have told you these things so that in me you may have peace. In this world you will have trouble. But take heart! I have overcome the world." I believe that students can thrive even

---

45. Hoy and Sweetland, "Designing Better Schools."
46. Goddard and Goddard, "Multilevel Analysis."
47. Hoy and Sweetland, "Designing Better Schools," 429.
48. Pepler, "Bullying Interventions."

in the midst of trauma and adversity. The purpose of resilience-informed teaching is for students to thrive.

Effective teaching means equipping all students with the three dimensions of thriving. First, students need to continually develop their non-cognitive skills in and out of the classroom. Secondly, students need to relate to others by cultivating their relational capacities. Lastly, school should be a place that cooperatively aligns with the individual student's needs to support students' learning experiences as a single unit.

2

The CARING Model and Resilience-Informed Teaching

Those who trust in their riches will fall,
but the righteous will thrive like a green leaf.

(PROVERBS 11:28)

INTRODUCTION

APPROXIMATELY 85 PERCENT OF students report having experienced at least one traumatic event in their lifetime and 66–94 percent of college students report exposure to one or more traumatic events while in college.[1] In the classroom, teachers may encounter many students who experience diverse trauma and adversity in their lives through academic, financial, relational, as well as spiritual issues. For example, during the COVID-19 pandemic, students' social, emotional, and mental well-being have been seriously impacted and it could continue to affect them in the future.

However, the purpose of education is to thrive in three areas, including personal, relational, and cultural dimensions. In order to implement thriving, I recommend resilience-informed teaching, which consists of six components that I will explain in more detail. First, I will address the key

---

1. Cless and Nelson-Goff, "Teaching Trauma"; Carello and Butler, "Practicing What We Teach."

points of resilience-informed teaching. Then, I will explain eight cases in the Beatitudes where Jesus implements a resilience-informed education. These eight cases will represent students in the classroom who experience trauma and adversity. Finally, I will introduce the CARING model for teachers to implement resilience-informed teaching, especially for traumatized students to help them to overcome and thrive.

WHAT IS RESILIENCE-INFORMED EDUCATION?

Education consists of intentional interventions to help all students thrive throughout their life. Trauma refers to emotionally or physically harmful events that damage our ability to function across social, emotional, behavioral, or physical domains.[2] A direct translation of the Greek word *trauma* is "wound" or "hurt."

Up to two-thirds of U.S. children have experienced at least one type of serious childhood trauma, such as abuse, neglect, natural disaster, or experiencing or witnessing violence.[3] Traumatized students are likely to frighten easily, experience anxiety in unfamiliar situations, and be clingy, difficult to soothe, aggressive, and/or impulsive. Jennings[4] identifies that students who are exposed to chronic trauma may be impaired in three key skills: a strong parent-child relationship; good cognitive skills; and the ability to self-regulate emotions, attention, and behaviors. The impact of trauma on learning is severe, as Wilpow et al.[5] summarizes it below:

- Traumatic stress can undermine the ability of children to form relationships, regulate their emotions, and learn the cognitive skills necessary to succeed academically.

- Students with symptoms of trauma may be unable to process verbal/nonverbal and written academic information.

- Traumatized students struggle to use language to relate to people, often because they are unable to use language to articulate their emotional needs and feelings.

2. SAMHSA, *National Survey.*

3. CDC, *Fourth National Report.*

4. Jennings, "Teaching in a Trauma-Sensitive Classroom," 13.

5. Wilpow et al., *Heart of Learning*, 12–13.

- When a child does not feel safe expressing a preference without first accessing the mood of a potentially volatile parent, this child cannot fully develop a sense of self.

- Children affected by trauma have trouble with classroom transitions from one situation to another.

- Classroom behavioral adaptations to trauma include aggression, defiance, withdrawal, perfectionism, hyperactivity, reactivity, impulsiveness, and/or rapid and unexpected emotional swings.

Teachers need to know that trauma impacts students of all backgrounds, in all dimensions of their lives, and to recognize that there are signs and symptoms of trauma for students. There are indeed pathways and interventions for students to recover from trauma, by promoting predictability and consistency. Fallot and Harris[6] identify five principles to teach traumatized students effectively: safety, establishing trustworthiness, maximizing choice, maximizing collaboration, and prioritizing empowerment. Building an open and supportive educational climate in which students are encouraged to practice constructive coping is an effective strategy as well. These strategies are foundational interventions for resilience-informed teaching in which teachers equip students with social and emotional competencies[7] during the inquiry-based teaching process. I will explain resilience-informed teaching in the CARING process section of this chapter in more detail.

Beatitudes: Cases of Students who Experience Trauma

In the Beatitudes (Matthew 5:3–10), Jesus identifies eight groups of people who experience trauma, adversaries, difficulties, and problems, but he proclaims that they are blessed. A direct translation of the Greek word *trauma* is "wound" or "hurt." The Greek word that translates to "blessed" is *makarios*, which means good, happy, joy, fortunate, and prosperous. Jesus turns conventional wisdom upside down in the Beatitudes by considering the miserable, the meek, the poor, the humble, the mourning, and the persecuted and the reviled as happy. Even though they experience trauma and adversities, Jesus commends them as blessed. They are blessed even if

---

6. Fallot and Harris, "Creating Cultures."

7. Melnick and Marinez, *Preparing Teachers*; Crosby et al., "Social Justice Education."

they lack material possessions, lose their loved ones, and suffer in relationships. Teachers can demonstrate happiness and prosperity for traumatized students in spite of their trauma and adversity, like Jesus in the Beatitudes. This is the essence of resilience-informed teaching, in which teachers help traumatized students thrive in their life by fulfilling their three dimensions in personal, relational, as well as cultural thriving.

In this chapter, there are eight cases of people who experience trauma along with rationales of why each of them are blessed. "Blessed are the poor in spirit, for theirs is the kingdom of heaven" (Matthew 5:3). People who experience physical as well as emotional and spiritual poverty, brokenness, and trauma may bring an acute understanding of themselves and their relationship with others, their work styles, and their strengths and weaknesses. Experiencing trauma and adversity makes people humble. Zacchaeus is one who was poor in spirit. He was isolated and bullied by his fellow Jews because of his outward appearance and his job as a tax collector in service to the enemy country. However, he thrived after he heard the teaching of Jesus. Likewise, there are many students who are bullied and suffer from physical, emotional, relational, and academic traumas like Zacchaeus. Resilience-informed teaching can be applied to this kind of student using the pedagogy of brokenness. I will explain this in chapter 3 more clearly.

The second category of people are those who are grieving due to the loss of a loved one or their dearest possessions.[8] Cleopas and the other disciple in Luke 24 mourned because they lost their master teacher, Jesus, who died on the cross. On the road to their hometown of Emmaus, however, Jesus transformed their hearts, which made them turn back to Jerusalem with confidence and enthusiasm. Their mourning turned into joy. Jesus proclaims: "Blessed are those who mourn, for they will be comforted" (Matthew 5:4). Likewise, many students experience trauma from poverty, family violence, loss of loved ones, etc. No matter what their situations are, the goal of resilience-informed teaching helps them thrive, instilling hospitality instead.

The third blessedness is for the meek. Jesus says, "Blessed are the meek, for they will inherit the earth" (Matthew 5:5). True meekness is achieved through humility and harmonious relationships with others, against the grain of human pride and self-seeking power. Jesus teaches the power of meekness to those who build an earthly kingdom through greed, injustice, and violence. Peter, although he is considered the chief apostle, remains

8. Hahn, *Matthew.*

impulsive and prideful and denies his master three times in John 18. While he was deeply traumatized with damaged emotions, Jesus came to him, accepting him and restoring the relationships that made Peter meek. Peter later recommended other Christians to be equipped with meekness (1 Peter 3:15). Likewise, many students share their traumatic experiences with their colleagues, parents, teachers, and significant others. How do we teach these students? In chapter 5, I will introduce the resilience-informed teaching process, focusing on healing memories with acceptance and attunement.

The fourth beatitude is for "those who hunger and thirst for righteousness." Righteousness is to release, vindicate, and reestablish a right relationship. There are many cases in the Bible where Jesus teaches and heals people with disabilities to establish the shalom relationship as God originally intended (Luke 7:13; Matthew 9:36; 15:32; Mark 6:34). For example, Jesus heals an invalid who had struggled for thirty-eight years at Bethesda by respectfully engaging with him (John 5:1–15). Jesus says, "Blessed are those who hunger and thirst for righteousness, for they will be filled" (Matthew 5:6). Resilience-informed teaching instills traumatized students with hope, resists learned helplessness, and boosts positive actions, which helps students with disabilities switch the thinking cycle from learned helplessness to learned hopefulness.

The next beatitude is about mercy. Mercy encompasses the ideas of both compassion and forgiveness.[9] Mercy is to suffer alongside, to fully enter the situation of the other, sharing in whatever comes together. In the Bible, Jesus criticizes the leaders of the Jews (the Pharisees, the Sadducees, and the teachers of the law) as hypocrites who see their neighbors as including only their fellow Jews, not extending mercy. In Luke 10:25–37, Jesus taught a self-righteous and prejudiced teacher of the law through the Parable of the Good Samaritan to be generous to all by showing love without partiality or preconditions. Jesus says, "Blessed are the merciful, for they will be shown mercy" (Matthew 5:7). How can we teach students who have been marginalized? In chapter 7, I will explain another case of resilience-informed teaching, utilizing culturally responsive education.

The sixth beatitude is about purity, which requires integrity, honesty, trust, and transparency.[10] Thomas, even though he was stigmatized as doubtful, was pure in heart. He didn't see his master when Jesus appeared to other disciples. His statement "unless I see the nail marks . . . I will not

---

9. Hahn, *Matthew*, 86.

10. Gill, "Eight Traits."

believe" (John 20:25) is not an expression of doubt, but a strong desire to see Jesus for himself. Healthy doubt should be valued in teaching because it makes learning more meaningful. Jesus answered Thomas by showing his wounds, leading Thomas into genuine worship. Matthew 5:8 says, "Blessed are the pure in heart, for they will see God."

Teachers may be exposed to students who are full of skepticism and doubt. I recommend using reasoned inquiry to promote students' critical thinking. In chapter 8, I will explain resilience-informed scaffolding strategies by using the CARING process.

The seventh beatitude, "Blessed are the peacemakers, for they will be called children of God" (Matthew 5:9), is about peacemakers. In a fallen world, quarreling and conflict arise whenever people suppress diversity and difference. Even among the twelve disciples of Jesus, there was much rivalry, each arguing who would be greater than the others. Jesus teaches them to demonstrate servant leadership by humbly serving others in order to be great. Likewise, some students are traumatized due to competition and rivalry. In chapter 8, I will introduce another model of resilience-informed teaching that emphasizes community actualization through humility.

The final beatitude is about social justice. Jesus says, "Blessed are those who are persecuted because of righteousness, for theirs is the kingdom of heaven" (Matthew 5:10). In the Bible, many people are marginalized, mistreated, and victimized due to cultural, linguistic, and racial disparities. For example, a Samaritan woman at a well faces severe discrimination by Jews in John 4. However, Jesus meets her, teaching her through discovery learning, which transforms her life, as she runs back to her village with a joyful heart. Likewise, there are many students in classrooms who are discriminated against due to race, ethnicity, gender, language, and religion. How can we teach this kind of marginalized student? In chapter 10, I will introduce equity pedagogy, another form of resilience-informed teaching, where educational and social inequality and unjust treatment are removed.

The Beatitudes give many insights for teachers on effective teaching procedures and classroom management strategies on teaching students who experience trauma and adversity along with ideas for building reliable educational environments. Gill summarizes:

> It was a needy, hurting and confused crowd [students] that Jesus saw. His response to this need was to call together a small community and work on rebuilding their character (individual) and culture (collectively, their community). This is the first lesson for

Christians who want to impact the needy crowds of our marketplace and world.[11]

The table below is a summary of eight cases related to traumatized students that are mentioned in the Beatitudes (Matthew 5). This resilience-informed teaching can be applied to any student who experiences trauma and adversity in order to help him/her thrive. You may read each case of the student in the coming chapters (chapters 3–10).

Table 2.1: Eight Traumatized Student Cases and Resilience-Informed Teaching

Cases in Beatitudes	Trauma Students Experience	Resilience-Informed Teaching Strategies
The poor in spirit (Matthew 5:3)	Students who are bullied and isolated	The pedagogy of brokenness by identifying students' inner pain and suffering
Those who mourn (Matthew 5:4)	Students who grieve due to losing their loved ones and hopes	Teaching students by demonstrating hospitality using revelatory affirmation
The meek (Matthew 5:5)	Students who experience damaged emotions and feelings	Providing healing with acceptance and attunement
Those who hunger and thirst (Matthew 5:6)	Students with physical disabilities and hopelessness	Switching the thinking cycle from learned helplessness to learned hopefulness
The merciful (Matthew 5:7)	Students who have been marginalized due to cultural prejudices	Offering culturally responsive teaching by promoting educational equity
The pure in heart (Matthew 5:8)	Students who doubt and are skeptic	Promoting their pure doubt and skepticism using reasoned inquiry

11. Gill, "Eight Traits," 616.

The peacemakers (Matthew 5:9)	Students who are prideful and rivalry	Initiating community-actualization education, utilizing paradox and reflexive thinking
Those who are persecuted (Matthew 5:10)	Students who are discriminated against due to gender and religious differences	Implementing equity pedagogy and social justice education

CARING PROCESS OF RESILIENCE-INFORMED TEACHING

In this section, I address six components of resilience-informed teaching, called CARING. In pursuing the exemplary case, I reflect the teaching of Jesus, who demonstrates the model of teaching that helps all audiences who experience trauma to thrive. You may find more strategies of resilience-informed teaching for students who experience diverse trauma in the following chapters. Jesus is the master teacher who demonstrates effective resilience-informed teaching, and I introduce some of his strategies here based on the CARING process. Teachers may use this framework to teach students who experience trauma in order to help them to overcome trauma.

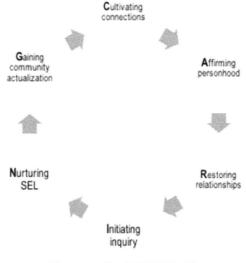

Figure 2.1: The CARING Model

Cultivating Connections

Every situation can mark an effective moment for teaching students about new concepts and subjects. Even if it is an unplanned occasion, teachers may use specific moments to introduce or expand upon something they want students to learn. Unexpected moments foster great connections with students. Veteran teachers have keen sensitivity to identify an apt moment to teach a particular topic with certain objects, contexts, and resources. Teaching is not a unilateral activity; it is rather bidirectional communication. Good teachers possess a capacity for connectedness.[12] Effective teaching begins when teachers get to know students' needs and assets and connect them to the topics they teach in the class. Education is not a one-size-fits-all, but tailored instruction to meet each individual student's diverse needs. Jesus is a differentiated instructor. He never uses the same strategies in situations. He uses diverse methods in order to meet each student's specific context. In order to connect with students, employ the following several strategies.

First, teachers may get to know each student's needs and assets in terms of cultural, linguistic, and family background and context. Why is Jesus' teaching so impactful? He contextualized his teaching by connecting with the audience. He used resources that were relevant to the audiences' lives, such as birds, lilies, a wineskin, a storm, taxes, a tunic, mustard seeds, sheep, goats, boats, nets, fish, little children, and a Roman coin. Teachers must respect the individuality, uniqueness, and personal worth of each person and incorporate the learners' developmental needs, ideas, and cultural context into the learning experience.

Second, teachers should hold high expectations for all students. Teachers' beliefs about their students critically influence their students' academic behaviors and achievement.[13] Why is Jesus' teaching effective? He always interacted with all people using respect and care, holding high expectations, and providing quality educational interventions that fit each situation.

Third, teachers should provide appropriate motivational strategies to meet each student's unique needs. In order to motivate students, teachers

---

12. Palmer, *Courage to Teach*.

13. Ruble-Davies, *Becoming a High Expectation Teacher*; Rosenthal and Jacobson, *Pygmalion in the Classroom*.

need to think about three elements of motivation factors: novelty, relevance, and emotion.[14]

Affirming Personhood

The goal of education is to restore the world to what God originally created it to be and to regain the relationship between Creator and creatures. Teachers need to recognize the truth that all humans are created in the image of God and possess inherent dignity and worth, and they need to have a unique respect for students' lives. Sadly, however, students' divine images are disconnected from the cold classroom reality where students are judged based on academic achievement and mistreated based on stereotyped expectations.[15] Kitwood defines personhood as "a standing or status that is bestowed upon one human being, by others, in the context of relationship and social being."[16] It implies recognition, respect, and trust. In fact, the term *personhood* is an essential characteristic of human beings, giving to us a universal worth and an exceptional standing.[17] If students who have experienced trauma, self-blame, self-harm, and isolation, this negatively impacts their identity and sense of hope.

Therefore, teachers need to affirm the personhood of each student through words and deeds. Affirmation refers to acknowledging each student and appreciating all cultural contexts that have been negated by dominant ideological frameworks.[18] How can teachers affirm students' unique features in the classroom? Teachers need to confront racial and cultural prejudice, bias, and discrimination existing in learning environments. Teachers need to accept all children by building a safe and trusted learning environment. When they are accepted, students see themselves as strong and build a social map that leads to a much better adulthood.[19]

Therefore, resilience-informed teaching is an act of social justice education. Resilience-informed teaching asks all teachers to abide by the foundational tenets: 1) awareness of the privilege and disempowerment that unequally exists across groups of people in our society, 2) recognition of

14. Hammond, *Culturally Responsive Teaching*, 48.

15. Pate, *Innocent Classroom*.

16. Kitwood, *Dementia Reconsidered*, 8.

17. White, "Personhood."

18. Hammond, *Culturally Responsive Teaching*.

19. Gabarino, *Raising Children*.

the prevailing power held by the dominant group and its pervasive impact on all systems within society, and 3) commitment to lifelong reflection on the ways in which we perpetuate oppression and actively working against it.[20]

Restoring Relationships

As Palmer[21] mentions, education involves building relationships between the known (the student) and the unknown (the subject) as the mediator between the two (the teacher). Resilience-informed teaching has identified the relationship between teacher and student as a key lever in fostering healing and hope. The previous stage, affirming personhood, is designed to recognize each student's worth and dignity, especially students who experience trauma. This stage acts to establish a safe and cooperative relationship between teacher and student, and student and student, productively and constructively. The purpose of this stage is for all students to thrive and feel safe in an environment where the expectations are clear and routines are predictable and consistent so that all students know what to expect.

Traditionally, teachers dominate the entire learning process, lecturing while students passively receive knowledge from the teacher. Nouwen[22] describes this kind of teaching as a violent process because it invokes three features: competitive, unilateral, and alienating. Freire[23] identifies the characteristics of the conventional education process as a banking education model in which teachers are considered the subject and students as passive objects. However, in resilience-informed education, building a trusting relationship between the teacher and students is critical. This kind of relationship is redemptive, evocative, bilateral, and actualizing.[24] This allows students to draw out their thoughts, feelings, and experiences in safe learning environments. In this way, both teacher and students search and learn bilaterally, actualizing the future into the present setting. In order to do that, a teacher's proximity always matters. Jesus' teaching starts when he approaches a specific audience, creating a space where students and Jesus

---

20. Crosby et al., "Social Justice Education," 16.

21. Palmer, *To Know as We Are Known.*

22. Nouwen, *Creative Ministry.*

23. Freire, *Pedagogy of the Oppressed.*

24. Nouwen, *Creative Ministry.*

freely discuss their challenges, trauma, and adversities. Fallot and Harris[25] identify several principles to restore relationships that provide respect and acceptance, including: 1) establishing and ensuring safety, 2) establishing trustworthiness, 3) maximizing choices, 4) maximizing collaboration, and 5) prioritizing empowerment.

Initiating Inquiry

Resilience-informed teaching promotes enrichment mindsets by fostering intellectual curiosity, emotional engagement, and social bonding.[26] In order to do that, teachers need to boost learning through a set of inquiries where students actively engage in learning sessions. Teachers may co-create a learning environment with students and their families, focusing on empowering students through shared decision-making and authentic choice. Jesus teaches his class using dialogues and inquiry, starting with essential questions, sharing parables and stories, checking for understanding (do you understand?), and allowing them to apply what they have learned. Lee and Freeman[27] identify three modes of teaching that Jesus uses and the table below is the summary of each mode.

Table 2.2: Three Modes of Teaching That Jesus Uses

Modes	Role of Teacher/ Learner	Learning Task	Biblical Examples
Guided inquiry	A teacher-centered Q&A process where learners are dependent on a teacher, but gain new understanding at the end of the inquiry	The learning task is academic and instructional. It should be understood via an inquiry led by a teacher	Disciples on the road to Emmaus (Luke 24), Nicodemus (John 3), the Samaritan woman at the well (John 4), a paralyzed man at Bethesda (John 5), the charcoal conversation with Peter (John 21)

25. Fallot and Harris, "Creating Cultures."
26. Leaf, *Think, Learn, Succeed*; Jensen, *Teaching with Poverty in Mind*.
27. Lee and Freeman, "Three Models."

Discovery learning	A teacher-led inquiry where learners are actively involved in the learning process; through the inquiry, the learners investigate issues and seek viable solution	The learning task is either an instructional or real task brought by a learner.	The story of the Prodigal Son (Luke 15), the Good Samaritan (Luke 10)
Problem-based learning	Learner-oriented problem-solving inquiry in which a teacher introduces a real problem that is to be solved by the learners	The learning task is a real, authentic task to be solved by students via collaboration.	Jesus sends disciples two by two (Matthew 10:1; Mark 6:7), disciples are asked to feed the crowd (John 6), the Great Commission (Matthew 28:19)

Nurturing SEL

Children who experience trauma often have difficulty regulating their emotions and disengage from school, which causes their academic performance to decline due to their lack of self-esteem.[28] Researchers have proven that students' social emotional capacities have significant effects on their academic outcomes as well as in their ability to thrive.[29]

Social and emotional learning (SEL) concerns the development of five emotional intelligence skills including: self-awareness, self-management, social awareness, relationship skills, and responsible decision-making.

- Self-awareness: recognizing and assessing one's emotions and thoughts and their influence on performance, behavior, confidence, and optimism;

- Self-management: regulating one's emotions, thoughts, and behaviors in various situations to effectively manage stress, impulses, motivation, and goal realization;

28. Steel, "Threat in the Air."

29. Ponton and Rhea, "Autonomous Learning"; Walton, "New Science"; Steiner-Adair, "Got Grit"; Olsen, *From Neuron to Neighborhood*.

- Social awareness: interacting socially, ethically, and empathetically with people of differing perspectives, cultures and backgrounds;

- Relationship skills: maintaining positive relationships with diverse individuals and groups by effectively communicating, listening, cooperating, negotiating and problem-solving;

- Responsible decision-making: using ethical standards, safety concerns, social norms, and the well-being of oneself and others when making choices.[30]

Displaying healthy social and emotional behaviors to traumatized students is essential because students who are exposed to trauma may suffer from a decreased ability to self-regulate their emotions, attention, and behavior.[31] How can teachers equip students with social-emotional capacities within their classroom contexts? Teachers may explicitly teach a set of socioemotional capacities (such as compassion and empathy) in class while they teach their content area. The following are just few examples of research about promoting students' social emotional capacities:

- Improving student social and emotional skills boosted test scores by eleven to seventeen points.[32]

- Students' psychosocial skills positively affected their academic success, supporting student goal alignment, feedback, resources, and skill development.[33]

- Students who underwent a social-emotional program performed about thirteen percentile points higher than their peers in the control group.[34]

- SEL not only improves achievement by an average of eleven percentile points, but it also increases prosocial behaviors (such as kindness, sharing, and empathy), improves student attitudes toward school, and reduces depression and stress among students.[35]

---

30. CASEL, *Framework*.
31. Jennings, "Teaching in a Trauma-Sensitive Classroom."
32. Durlark et al., "Impact of Enhancing Students' SEL."
33. Bandura, "Social Cognitive Theory"; Dweck, "Motivational Processes."
34. Blad, "Measuring the Social and Emotional."
35. Durlark et al., "Impact of Enhancing Students' SEL."

- Teaching students social and emotional skills decrease student misbehavior significantly.[36] Teachers should take care of students' social emotional well-being and mental health.

Gaining Community Actualization

Education is for actualizing each student's full capacities as well as actualizing the community to promote equity, equality, and justice. The goal of education is not only to strengthen each student's knowledge, skills, and competencies, but also to build a strong community together where all people are connected in unity. The Bible clearly depicts this image in Isaiah 11:6, where the lion and the lamb lie together. Building a sense of belonging is a basic human need in which we enable the ability to see value in life and cope with challenges.

Since Maslow shared the hierarchy of needs in 1943, American education has hyper-focused on individual prosperity. However, research proves that students do best in open, supportive educational climates that encourage constructive coping with problems in community.[37] Strengthening the educational community is particularly important for students who are experiencing trauma and adversity, especially those who are ethnically and culturally diverse, sexual minorities, developmentally delayed, as well as linguistically diverse. How do teachers promote a safe and trusted school community? In the previous chapter, I mentioned some strategies under the topic of "cultural thriveology." But in this section I will add two more strategies. First, we need to promote a collaborative school culture where students share, discuss, and work together in community. Gruenert and Whitaker[38] identify six types of school cultures, among which collaborative school culture is considered the most productive and effective type. Osterman[39] identifies the characteristics of a collaborative school culture as help, support, trust, openness, collective reflection, and collective efficacy. Therefore, teachers and administrators must work to redesign schools with stronger relationships where students do best in open, supportive educational climates that encourage constructive problem-coping. Kohm and

---

36. Mergler et al., "Alternative Discipline."
37. Garbarino, *Raising Children*; Hammond, *Culturally Responsive Teaching*.
38. Gruenert and Whitaker, *School Culture Rewired*.
39. Osterman, "Students' Need for Belonging."

Nance[40] also identify the major features of collaborative culture, such as: 1) teachers support one another's efforts to improve instruction; 2) teachers take responsibility for solving problems and accept the consequences of their decisions; 3) teachers share ideas. As one person builds on another's ideas, a new synergy develops; and 4) teachers evaluate new ideas in light of shared goals that focus on student learning.

In addition, establishing a socially harmonious classroom is another effective concept to implement.[41] It is conceptualized as a multilevel intervention that involves activities for the whole school community in which all students receive resilience-informed interventions, such as mindfulness, nonviolent communication, emotional processing, decision making, etc.

CONCLUDING REMARKS

After Jesus delivers the Beatitudes, he concludes the Sermon on the Mount by saying: "You are the light of the world . . . Let your light shine before others, that they may see your good deeds and glorify your Father in heaven" (Matthew 5:13–16). This is the responsibility of all teachers regardless of their content areas or which grades they teach. There are many students who are experiencing traumas and adversities in the classroom, and teachers need to make a positive impact through interventions. In the chapters that follow, I will identify traumatized students based on the eight beatitudes and explain how Jesus effectively teaches each person. His methods and strategies are still applicable to today's students because he taught as one who had authority and not as the teachers of the law (Matthew 7:29).

---

40. Kohm and Nance, "Creating Collaborative Cultures."
41. Haymovitz et al., "Exploring the Perceived Benefits."

3

Thriveology for the Bullied and Isolated Student

Blessed are the poor in spirit, for theirs is the kingdom of heaven.

(MATTHEW 5:3)

THE STORY OF ZACCHAEUS

THERE WAS A PERSON who was despised, bullied, and hated by his countrymen. No one wanted to associate with him, despite his riches and high
position of prestige. Instead, people pointed their fingers at him, criticizing
him as a traitor, extortionist, scumbag, and dirty old man.

His name was Zacchaeus. There remain two main reasons why he
was bullied and hated by others. First, he was not physically attractive. He
was short and had an unintimidating physical presence. There was noth-
ing in the appearance of the man to draw others to him, as shortness is
synonymous with narrow-minded thinking according to Jewish traditional
thought. Secondly, as a director of the revenue office for the Roman govern-
ment, his job was to extort money from his countrymen to pay taxes to
their greatest enemy. He also presided over other tax collectors and received
their collections. It was natural for tax collectors to be considered traitors
by fellow Jews. He was always alone and isolated. He had felt disdain when
he heard the insults of his countrymen while walking the streets. He had

been kicked out of the synagogue and shunned by his neighbors, much like the black sheep of the family. He must have lived in perpetual loneliness and self-pity.

However, in reality, Zacchaeus had not been happy with his practice of extorting undue tax money from his fellow country people. Even though he worked for another country, he felt his spiritual bankruptcy and emotional drainage, leading him to seek transparency and integrity. The meaning of his name is "pure." He heard that Jesus taught people like him with deep compassion and love, demonstrating a new way of life without judging people based on their career, physical appearance, and external contexts. He was motivated to meet Jesus. Finally, he heard that Jesus was coming to his village and decided to see who Jesus was.

WHEN JESUS TEACHES THE POOR IN SPIRIT

When Jesus stopped by Bethany, Zacchaeus's hometown, many people came out to see him. Zacchaeus was there as well; however, he couldn't see Jesus over the crowd because of his short stature. He wanted to see and meet Jesus, but the crowd would not let him through. Desperate and anxious, he climbed a sycamore fig tree. Finally, he could see Jesus clearly.

Did Jesus know the heart of Zacchaeus? Of course, the master teacher knew it. Effective teaching begins even before class officially starts. Teachers know how each student prepares their hearts for each class. Like Zacchaeus, attending class with eagerness and the aspiration to learn something from the teacher are key factors for success. A master teacher's competency depends on their awareness of how much each student prepares for class even before the class begins.

How can we know this? There are two ways to ascertain students' preparedness. First, teachers may use a diagnostic assessment at the beginning of the class. Teachers may ask a couple of questions to students to understand how ready students are. However, a more powerful method would be to promote students' intrinsic motivation, which can be identified using three characteristics: students' internal sense of control, their competence to control learning challenges, and connecting learning to their contexts.[1] Students' internal sense of control, their ability to self-direct behavior and attitude, and desires and interests to pursue goals are critically important

---

1. Dweck and Leggett, "Social-Cognitive Approach"; Ryan and Deci, "Intrinsic and Extrinsic Motivations."

to direct a positive achievement outcome. Jesus' teaching was powerful to audiences except for the Pharisees and teachers of the law because of the differences in their motivations and attitudes. People like Zacchaeus were intrinsically motivated to hear Jesus' message even before they came to him. The effective teacher has keen competencies to know students' hearts and desires and promotes their intrinsic motivation to accomplish their learning goals.

Jesus was passing by when Zacchaeus was waiting. When Jesus reached the spot, he looked up at him. Teachers acknowledge their students' seeking heart and students feel their teacher's loving, tender acceptance. Powerful teaching consists of many logical connections throughout the lesson. Psychologist Cziksentmihalyi[2] calls this an optimal experience "flow." This refers to a specific occasion where students feel a sense of exhilaration, a deep sense of enjoyment that becomes a landmark in their lives. This was an unforgettable life experience for Zacchaeus.

The crowds were curious, awaiting his message. Jesus' eyes, however, focused on one person. The crowd remained skeptical, and there was only one person who was truly desperate to see Jesus. This is the starting point of powerful teaching. The purpose of education is to ignite students' hearts. While students come to class with ready minds, teachers must seek to connect with those who are ready. When Jesus looked up at him, Zacchaeus looked down into the face of the Teacher. This genuine connection ignites and invites effective, authentic learning.

Jesus called his name: "Zacchaeus." Maybe this was the first time he was called by name. Zacchaeus may have been surprised. Somebody knew his name and called out to him personally. Someone knew of his situation, his needs, and his heart. Real education can begin at the moment there is trust between teacher and student. In order to build trust, a teacher needs to get to know their students' needs, assets, and cultural, linguistic, and family background. Jesus knew that Zacchaeus had searched for the way to be redeemed, to be eagerly freed from all the stigmatized images given by his fellow country people. Notice the first thing Jesus said to the man on the limb: "Zacchaeus." Jesus knows human beings by name. Notice that Jesus did not say, "Zacchaeus, you're a sinner; you've been ripping people off." Jesus spoke to this chief tax collector with words of frankness, but surely with kindness.

2. Cziksentmihalyi, *Flow.*

"Zacchaeus, come down immediately. I must stay at your house today" (Luke 19:5–6). This is called the zone of proximal development. Education starts to draw students in a tangible and manageable distance where learners can actively participate in learning activities. Vygotsky refers to this as "the distance between the actual developmental level as determined by independent problem solving and the level of potential development as determined through problem-solving under adult guidance, or in collaboration with more capable peers."[3] The distance between Jesus and Zacchaeus was too far when Zacchaeus stayed on the branch of the sycamore tree. When Jesus called to him, the zone of proximal development was formed; he was provided appropriate assistance by the teacher. As long as the zone of proximal development is formed, effective education may take place. There is no hindrance. Think about the words "immediately," "today," and "at once." Zacchaeus made haste, came down from the tree, and received Jesus joyfully. Jesus' message breathes hope into the soul of a wayward sinner and gives meaning and excitement to one's life.

Now, a face-to-face class begins. Jesus asked to have dinner with him at his house that day (Luke 19:10). The teacher not only recognized the student's heart and desire; he wanted to be with him in spite of all he knew about Zacchaeus's unsavory reputation. When Jesus and Zacchaeus walked home together, the uncaring crowds hissed and jeered, saying, "He has gone to be a guest with a man that is a sinner" (Luke 19:7). Those who murmured were undoubtedly the Pharisees, the other group of teachers at that time, who abandoned all care for their students.

We don't know how Jesus taught the audience in Zacchaeus's house. Certainly there was much discussion and prayer; questions and answers would follow. Zacchaeus may have had a heavy heart during the discourse led by Jesus, making way for a serious confrontation of his unsatisfying, greedy lifestyle. The reason why the teaching of Jesus was amazing (Mark 1:22, Luke 4:32) was his teaching style. Unlike the Pharisees and other Jewish teachers, who primarily focused on repetition so their learners would remember their teaching verbatim, Jesus was interested in changing mindsets through discovery. Jesus emphasized reasoning, listening, and asking questions.[4] His teaching was usually aided through dialogue, inquiry, and discussion, where students were actively engaged in the learning process.

---

3. Vygotsky, *Mind in Society*, 86.
4. Lee, "Jesus' Teaching through Discovery"; Burbules, "Jesus as a Teacher."

While students are participating in the learning, they reflect and check their inner worldviews, perspectives, and viewpoints.

The powerful result of this teaching was that Zacchaeus applied his learning from Jesus to inform his life in practical ways. Immediately, there was a dramatic change in his life. He suddenly stood up and promised to pay back what he had wrongfully collected from others. His passion to hoard was replaced with a passion to give. His grip on material things was loosened, and he was ready to give away much of his fortune.

What is the result of teaching in this situation? Before summarizing the effectiveness of Jesus' teaching at this time, we need to check the biblical framework. There are three components of growth: knowledge, understanding, and wisdom. Paul suggests in Colossians 2:9: "We continually ask God to fill you with the knowledge of his will through all the wisdom and understanding that the Spirit gives." Students need to grow in knowledge so that they can grasp principles. Furthermore, students need to practice what they have learned to transform their behaviors and situations, which is called wisdom.

FOUR LEVELS OF EVALUATION

How can we evaluate the effectiveness of Jesus' teaching? One of the best-known models for analyzing and evaluating the results of an educational program is the Kirkpatrick model.[5] This model identifies four different levels of evaluation: reaction, learning, application, and impact.

Table 3.1: Four Levels of Evaluation

Levels	Purpose	Methods
1 (Reaction)	Measuring how learners react to the program (session)	Smile test, exit ticket, observation and interview
2 (Learning)	Measuring how learners meet the predefined learning goals	Comparing the pre- and post-test scores, interview, observations, summative assessment

5. Kirkpatrick and Kirkpatrick, *Evaluating Training Programs.*

| 3 (Behavior) | Measuring how learners changed in behavior by utilizing what they learned in their situations | Comprehensive observation, interviews, a 360 evaluation (usually conducts three to six months after the program) |
| 4 (Impact) | Measuring how learners made a positive impact on their belonged organizations | Statistical analysis using control and experimental groups, return-on-investment (ROI) analysis |

The reaction evaluation (Level 1) measures students' attitudes and reactions about the particular training program, asking how engaged students were, how actively students contributed and how they reacted to the lesson. Zacchaeus was joyous and full of happiness when Jesus looked up to him, called him, and asked him to stay at his house. His outcome of the reaction evaluation would be highly effective.

The next level is the learning evaluation, which focuses on measuring what students have learned. Through the teaching of Jesus, Zacchaeus learned the principles of new life, freedom, and salvation from his previous bounded lifestyle. He was now saved and became a child of Abraham. The Level 3 evaluation is to change students' behaviors by applying what they have learned to their particular situations and contexts. Because of the teaching of Jesus, Zacchaeus was changed and applied this change to his life. He boldly proclaimed: "Here and now I am giving half of my possessions to the poor!" He also promised to return whatever he had taken falsely from others, and he would give back four times the amount he had wrongfully taken. The power of the teaching of Jesus lies in application. That's why Jesus criticized the Pharisees and teachers of the law as hypocrites, because they did not apply what they taught. However, the teachings of Jesus were full of cases where his students applied what they learned from him to their situations.

Finally, the Level 4 evaluation is the results evaluation. This includes outcomes that impact the community to which students belong. Jesus proclaimed, "Today salvation has come to this house." Zacchaeus's restitution to those he has harmed or cheated positively impacts his community. The teaching of Jesus powerfully infiltrates all four levels of evaluation, which is a powerful lesson from a master teacher.

PEDAGOGY OF BROKENNESS

The story of Zacchaeus shows us that even people who have lost their integrity can find it again through insightful teaching by an effective teacher. Zacchaeus represents students who are isolated, bullied, and hated by fellow students. Like Zacchaeus, there are many students in the classroom who are marginalized. They are alone both inside and outside of the classroom. Teachers remain key motivators for them to transform their lives. Students who are experiencing trauma and adversity have an inner desire to grow only when they are invested in, when their unique assets and needs are seen and acknowledged. Jesus' effective teaching led Zacchaeus to reflect upon his life and to make a responsible decision.

The important role of a teacher is to identify students who are experiencing trauma and see their broken hearts and emotions, which I call "the pedagogy of brokenness." The pedagogy of brokenness ascribes to go deeper to identify students' pain and suffering from physical, emotional, relational, financial, and academic traumas they have experienced as well as spiritual brokenness. As Jesus showed in this case, teachers need to demonstrate joy, hope, and peace in the midst of broken experiences. How do we demonstrate the pedagogy of brokenness to teach students who experience trauma? Using the CARING model, teachers may utilize the following procedures when teaching.

Cultivating Connections

When nobody wanted to befriend Zacchaeus, only Jesus called him by name. Jesus fully understood his long suffering and isolation from his community, who judged him as a traitor and sinner. When Jesus looked up at him, he recognized Zacchaeus's inner heart and desire to be part of an authentic community with other fellow Jews. The crowd despised him, but Jesus lifted his attention to Zacchaeus and called his name. Making a personal connection by calling one's name is the starting point of effective teaching. How do we make connections with students who are experiencing trauma and adversity and open the door for building trust? Hammond[6] identifies several strategies, called "Trust Generators," including:

- Selective vulnerability: sharing teachers' vulnerable moments;

6. Hammond, *Culturally Responsive Teaching*, 79.

- Familiarity: developing a sense of familiarity with students who they see often in a particular setting;

- Similarity of interests: sharing likes, dislikes, hobbies, sports that are similar to students' interest;

- Concern: showing concerns for those issues and events (such as births, illnesses, life transitions) important to students;

- Competence: demonstrating skills, knowledge, and will to support students.

Affirming Personhood

Because he had served the enemy country, Zacchaeus lived in isolation, which negatively impacted his identity. However, Jesus truly believed that Zacchaeus was a son of Abraham. Far too often, people make judgments about others based on how they look or act. Jesus, however, does not judge people based on outward appearance, but always looks at the heart (1 Samuel 16:7), because all people are created in the image of God. There are some students in the classroom who have experienced many kinds of trauma and find that those lifestyles are meaningless and hollow. The responsibility of the teacher is to accept all students equally and equitably, providing a safe learning environment where students feel at home and actively participate in learning activities.

To promote healing and learning, teachers must support students with developing their positive self-perception and model an overall attitude of hope through specific language and competence. Students who are experiencing trauma must build a strong, healthy perception of themselves. For them, self-blame, self-harm, and isolation negatively impacts their identity and sense of hope.[7] Therefore, the most impactful use of language is praise and attention. Good intentions, however, can unintentionally trigger trauma. If students affected by trauma perceive empty praise, it destroys trust.

How did Jesus ascertain Zacchaeus's personhood? He called his name. He asked to stay at his house. Jesus intentionally recognized his worthiness in front of the Pharisees, who condemned Zacchaeus as a sinner. Jesus confirmed that Zacchaeus was a member of Abraham's household. Teachers purposefully advocate for students' personhood.

7. Garbarino, "Educating Children."

Restoring Relationships

Students need a stable, positive emotional relationship with at least one adult or other reference person as personal anchors to navigate a successful school and life experience.[8] Zacchaeus struggled with the broken relationships with his fellow men. "Zacchaeus, hurry and come down, for I must stay at your house today." This was the first anchoring point that built a positive relationship with Zacchaeus. In addition, this caused Zacchaeus to extend positive relationships with others. How did Jesus make a positive relationship with Zacchaeus? First, Jesus demonstrated caring. Jesus' actions and words communicated that he sincerely cared for Zacchaeus. In order to demonstrate caring, Boynton and Boynton[9] suggest several strategies that teachers may utilize in their classroom, such as 1) listening intently and sincerely to students, 2) inquiring about aspects of students' personal lives, and 3) understanding the emotions behind an incident.

Second, maintaining proximity is another key method that Jesus used. "Zacchaeus . . . I must stay at your house today." Proximity gave Jesus a front-row seat to closely observe what happened and empathize with the pain and trauma that this student experienced. Sitting in the front row is a privilege, an opportunity to see what's really going on and allow those factors to penetrate the teacher's heart and mind, bringing them to a place where the teacher can participate in the transformation.[10] Jesus was willing to stay with the sinner, a traitor who was criticized by his fellow Jews. However, where there is no proximity, there is no transformation in students' hearts. Teachers need to be placed into a student's context, engaging in meaningful connections with their students.[11]

Initiating Inquiry

Scripture doesn't explain in detail how Jesus taught the crowds at Zacchaeus's house. However, one thing is certain. Jesus didn't teach by asking people to memorize the law or recite the Jewish statute. He never spoon-fed his students. Jesus probably led discussions or shared regarding the matter

---

8. Garbarino, "Educating Children."

9. Boynton and Boynton, *Educator's Guide*.

10. Warren, *Power of Proximity*, 16.

11. Assor et al., "Choice Is Good."

of restitution for past sins. This inquiry deeply moved Zacchaeus so that finally he was willing to restore four times over to those he wronged.

Nurturing SEL

Social and emotional learning (SEL) enhances students' ability to succeed in school, career, and life. There are five areas of SEL: self-awareness, self-management, social awareness, relationship skills, and responsible decision-making. The teaching of Jesus to Zacchaeus was impactful because it caused Zacchaeus to grow his social emotional capacities. For example, he accurately recognized his own emotions, thoughts, and values and how they influenced his behavior (self-awareness). He persevered even though the crowds sneered at him by regulating his emotions and behaviors (self-management). He clearly emphasized and felt compassion for those people he wronged when he collected taxes (social awareness). Now, he could establish and maintain healthy relationships with others, especially with those who criticized and mocked him (relationship skills). Finally, he could make a responsible decision to repay the people he had wronged.

Gaining Community Actualization

Jesus concluded his teaching from focusing on one person to the whole community. He said, "Today salvation has come to this house, because this man, too, is a son of Abraham. For the Son of Man came to seek and save the lost" (Luke 19:9–10). We do not know the future of this story; however, we expect that Zacchaeus would be accepted as a community member by his fellow citizens to build a collaborative community together.

CONCLUDING REMARKS

Teachers can change one student's life as well as transform the community and world. This is the power of effective teaching. This kind of teaching is still effective in contemporary classrooms, where many students struggle with trauma and toxic environments so that they become bullied, isolated, and marginalized.

4

Thriveology for Grieving Students

Blessed are those who mourn, for they will be comforted

(MATTHEW 5:4)

THE STORY OF TWO DISCIPLES WHO MOURNED

TWO DISCIPLES OF JESUS, Cleopas and his unnamed companion, were in deep grief because their master, who was called the Messiah, was crucified. When they were together with Jesus, they witnessed the many miracles and wonders that their teacher performed. They thought Jesus would be the one to redeem Israel from their oppressor, the Roman Empire. However, they instead confronted the reality of their teacher being shamefully arrested and put to death on the cross. They lost all hope and left Jerusalem for Emmaus, their hometown. However, on the road to Emmaus, the pitiable travelers met the risen Jesus, who led them to inquiry through hospitality. They learned Scriptures from their teacher, which gave them reason to regain hope and confidence, as they decided to return to Jerusalem with enthusiasm and great joy. Why was his teaching so effective? What made them transform their hearts and minds so drastically? This is the power of hospitality.

JESUS' TEACHING WITH HOSPITALITY

The disciples had expected Jesus to unmistakably defeat their oppressors and fulfill their dreams. Read what they said in Luke 24:21: "We had hoped that he was the one who was going to redeem Israel." But the exact opposite appears to have happened. The disciples saw their teacher arrested and sentenced to death on a cross like a common criminal. All their hopes were dashed and the disciples all mourned deeply. The Bible says in Luke 24:17, "they stood still, their faces downcast." Finally, two disciples left Jerusalem to travel to their hometown of Emmaus for Passover, probably tormented by their traumatized hopes, broken dreams, and disappointments along the way.

Suddenly, Jesus joined their journey as an unrecognizable figure, showing the hospitality that God offers to mourners. Jesus taught the two disciples by leading dialogue through which they gained new insights on Scripture. Finally, they returned to Jerusalem with enthusiasm and joyful hearts. Jesus demonstrated effective strategies of hospitality to those who mourn in this situation, showing why practicing hospitality is crucial to teaching.

JESUS: THE HOSPITABLE TEACHER

First, Jesus provided a space of hospitality to those who were deeply mourning. Sometimes it is hard to intervene with mourners who have lost their beloved one. Hospitality is key to intercede in the lives of students who are deeply discouraged. Hospitality means to empathize with a person's struggles and pains with openness and care.[1] God commanded the Israelites to welcome others who experience deep struggles and difficulties (Deuteronomy 1:16–17). Teachers may see many students in the classroom who encounter diverse forms of trauma, pain, and suffering. To them, classrooms should be a place to practice hospitality. In order to do that, teachers need to create a free space where students can enter the classroom and become active participants instead of outsiders. Teachers are to create a welcoming space, a friendly emptiness where all students can enter and discover themselves as creations and allow them to freely sing, dance, play, and speak in their own styles, cultures, and languages.[2]

1. Palmer, *Promise of Paradox*.
2. Nouwen, *Reaching Out*.

Palmer[3] identifies six paradoxical tensions to build into the teaching and learning space, which are neither prescriptive nor exhaustive. They are: 1) the space should be bounded and open; 2) the space should be hospitable and charged; 3) the space should invite the voice of the individual and the voice of the group; 4) the space should honor the little stories of the students and the big stories of disciplines and tradition; 5) the space should support solitude and surround itself with the resources of community; and 6) the space should welcome both silence and speech.

"What are you discussing together as you walk along?" (Luke 24:17). "What things?" (Luke 24:19). These two questions that Jesus asked to those whose faces were downcast served as signs that opened a hospitable space where he and two disciples could freely talk. When a teacher creates a free and friendly space, hostility is converted to hospitality and fearful strangers can become guests revealing to their hosts the promise they are carrying with them.[4] In the hospital classroom, there comes a new sense of unity between the teacher and students, in which students and teachers are co-investigators.[5] This learning process, which stresses the learners' experience and expression, reverses the traditional top-down model of teaching (banking), in which the one who knows (the teacher) imparts knowledge to one who is presumed ignorant (the student). In the hospitable classroom, students and teachers can enter into a fearless communication with each other and allow their respective life experiences to be their primary and most valuable source of growth and maturation.

Hospitality: Revealing and Affirming

"What things?" As a hospitable teacher, Jesus let the disciples share their feelings, emotions, and experiences in the safe learning space. While Jesus heard what they said, he kept silent and allowed them to share the stories they wanted to tell. Nouwen summarizes hospitality-based dialogue as identified by two aspects: revealing and affirming.[6] The teacher has to reveal to the students that they have something to offer, so the teacher has to first reveal, to take away the veil covering many students' intellectual lives, and help them see that their own life experiences, their own insights,

3. Palmer, *Courage to Teach*.

4. Nouwen, *Reaching Out*, 47.

5. Freire, *Pedagogy of the Oppressed*.

6. Nouwen, *Reaching Out*, 62.

convictions, intuitions, formations are worth serious attention. Teachers detach themselves from their need to impress and control by allowing themselves to become receptive to their students. Then, the hospitable teacher affirms (encouragement, support). The teacher helps students to clarify their hidden motives, competencies, and knowledge by helping them develop and deepen them so that they can continue renewing their self-confidence from self-doubt.

Hospitality-based education requires teachers to have a humble and empathetic attitude. Students are not poor, needy, ignorant beggars who ask teachers to fill their empty vessels. They are the image-bearers of God who are equipped with sound capacities and abilities to be fully actualized through quality interactions with hospitable teachers. Remember the powerful effect of hospitality in this case. After they invited Jesus to their home at Emmaus, the roles were reversed. The stranger, Jesus, became the host, while the hosts became his learners. Now, the real teaching begins.

What is the result of effective teaching? This learning experience resulted in immediate action. After learning from the teacher, they made the seven-mile return journey to Jerusalem, where they shared the good news of what they had learned with the eleven disciples. Jesus was alive and appeared to them on the road (Luke 24:33–35). When we teach, we hope that students apply what they learn and live out of their new understandings of God's kingdom. Christian teachers seek to facilitate a transforming encounter with the living Christ that leads to new ways of acting, thinking, and feeling.

CARING TEACHING PROCEDURE: TEACHING AS AN ACT OF HOSPITALITY

While teaching, teachers may encounter diverse cases with students in their professional journeys. Like Jesus, who came along the road to Emmaus and met two disciples who mourned over the loss of their master, teachers may confront many students in and out of classrooms who have unique life stories. Some may experience trauma or adversity; some may struggle with family violence; some students come to school hungry; some are mourning over the loss of their loved ones; some have lost their future, etc. The road to Emmaus is thus the road traveled by people who experience many stories, and the same goes for students.

Therefore, teaching is an act of hospitality in which teachers welcome strangers or newcomers who enter the classroom.[7] No matter what their situations are, teachers are to be change agents, bridging students' current situations to their bright futures and dreams. While they walk the road to Emmaus, teachers instill confidence, hope, and conviction in students through quality educational interventions. How can we teachers teach students like Jesus, who taught effectively and sent them back to their journeys confidently? Based on the CARING process, I will share some strategies for teaching students who mourn.

Cultivating Connections

Education is not confined to a school classroom. It can be held at any time and at any place. A long time ago, God told the Israelites through Moses about impactful teaching strategies: "talk about them when you sit at home and when you walk along the road, when you lie down and when you get up" (Deuteronomy 6:7). Think about Jesus, who silently walked alongside them, listening to what they discussed. They wanted to know what was going on and understand the turn of events. They were so preoccupied with discussing what had happened in Jerusalem that they didn't recognize Jesus was among them. Meanwhile, Jesus also knew that they were deeply discouraged and grieved. However, they couldn't comprehend the things that had happened. So, Jesus intervened in order to teach that the death of Christ offers the greatest hope possible. Identifying students' needs even before the class starts is essential for effective teaching. Teachers need to collect students' data through a diagnostic assessment process.

A learning space should be hospitable not in order to make learning painless, but to make the painful learnings possible. Piaget[8] explains an effective learning process using the dynamic relationship between equilibrium and disequilibrium. When people come across ideas that conflict with their existing schema, disequilibrium occurs. Disequilibrium is a strong motivator to learn. Disequilibrium can be overcome by accepting a new idea or new knowledge. Jesus used questions to inspire audiences to formulate new schemas that challenged their existing framework of ideas. By providing a learning space, Jesus allowed two disciples to expose their

7. Gallagher, "Welcoming the Stranger."
8. Piaget, *Equilibrium of Cognitive Structures.*

ignorance, test tentative hypotheses, challenge false or partial information, and develop mutual criticisms of thought.

Affirming Personhood

Students bring diverse backgrounds to the classroom. They are different racially, ethnically, culturally, and religiously. The role of teachers is to provide a safe and hospitable environment in order to weave students' differences in the learning community of shalom where all students grow to their fullest potential. Therefore, hospitality is the practice of welcoming students who are unknown into a space that has meaning and value for them because all are created in the image of God.[9]

In order to provide a hospitable pedagogy, the role of a teacher is to be a good host who values students and the perspectives they bring to the classroom by being attentive and listening.[10] When I read C. S. Lewis' book *The Lion, the Witch and the Wardrobe*, I was thrilled to gain insight about the hospitable teacher through Aslan. When Aslan was resurrected from the dead, he visited the witch's courtyard, where he woke up all dead, stone creatures. Lewis beautifully describes the scene:

> For a second after Aslan had breathed upon him the stone lion looked just the same. Then a tiny streak of gold began to run along his white marble back, then it spread, then the color seemed to lick all over him as the flame licks all over a bit of paper, then, while his hindquarters were still obviously stone, the lion shook his mane and all the heavy, stone folds rippled into living hair. Then he opened a great red mouth, warm and living, and gave a prodigious yawn. And now his hind legs had come to life. Then, having caught sight of Aslan, he went bounding after him and frisking round him whimpering with delight and jumping up to lick his face. . . . Everywhere the statues were coming to life. The courtyard looked no longer like a museum; it looked more like a zoo. Creatures were running after Aslan and dancing round him till he was almost hidden in the crowd.[11]

This is a typical example of a hospitable teacher. True education is to breathe living hope into learners, like Aslan did to the creatures. The dead,

9. Burwell and Huyser, "Practicing Hospitality."
10. Marmon, "Teaching as Hospitality."
11. Lewis, *Lion, the Witch*, 168.

stone bodies turned to the living creatures Lewis describes vividly. All of the statues in the witch's courtyard were revived again, so the courtyard no longer resembled a museum that was filled with the culture of silent death, but now it was a zoo where all creatures sing, dance, run, and jump with joy and happiness. How can we do that? By creating a hospitable classroom environment where teachers affirm each student's unique character and talents from God and allow them to self-actualize through quality education.

Restoring Relationships

One Bible passage that we must be attentive to is: "Jesus himself came up . . . " (Luke 24:15). He himself approached them, which means he personally was involved in their need. When students are perplexed, discouraged, and deep in mourning, the teacher herself comes to them to be with students. Even though a student's life may be painful, mournful, and full of trauma, it is the teacher who creates a free and fearless space where mental and emotional development can take place.[12] Yes, students can overcome the challenge as long as the teacher is present with a hospitable heart. This is the power of presence and proximity. Teachers draw near to students with love and comfort, which makes students succeed. Palmer[13] addresses teachers' capacities to respect and recognize students' needs:

- A respect for students' stories;
- A desire to help students build a bridge between the academic text and their own lives;
- An ability to see students' lives more clearly than they themselves see them;
- An aptitude for asking good questions and listening carefully to students' responses;
- A willingness to take risks, especially the risk of inviting open dialogue.

Demonstrating intellectual hospitality is essential in order to build a safe classroom environment where the host (teacher) welcomes strangers (students) who join the classroom with diverse backgrounds.[14] With lov-

12. Nouwen, *Reaching Out*.
13. Palmer, *Courage to Teach*, 71–72.
14. Gallagher, "Welcoming the Stranger."

ing and empathetic spirits, teachers need to care for each student equitably. Think about Jesus, who loved even Judas, who betrayed him. He eagerly took on the cross and died for all sinners. Jesus knew his disciples by name. In John 10:14 he said, "I am the good shepherd; I know my sheep and my sheep know me." "What are you discussing together as you walk along?" Didn't Jesus know the things that they discussed? He heard all that they discussed, but he wanted to be with them publicly, asking for their permission to stay with them. "What things?" There is humor and joy in his interaction, but Jesus was patient and didn't spoil the surprise because he didn't want to drop the truth on them. He gave them space to express their disappointment and the tension they were feeling. In order to develop a positive relationship with students who mourn, teachers must implement two things. First, teachers must provide a safe and hospitable space where students can express their feelings and emotions. Second, teachers must be a listening ear to them, allowing students to speak before interjecting. McHugh[15] identifies three teacher competencies to build a positive relationship, which are honesty, vulnerability, and intimacy.

Initiating Inquiry

Jesus provided a learning space for them where he listened silently to all their frustration before leading an inquiry. The inquiry learning model is learning that requires students to solve problems through investigation activities that increase their skills and knowledge independently.[16] Inquiry is a process to gain understanding by engaging students in open-ended and hands-on activities. An inquiry usually takes three steps 1) begin with a captivating question; 2) allow students to explore new insights and new learning; and 3) encourage students to apply what they have learned to their life settings.

Jesus asked them, "What are you discussing together as you walk along?" (Luke 24:17), which is the first stage of inquiry. Two disciples were discussing together, but the issues were too hard to comprehend. At the right time, Jesus intervened. The question of Jesus would be captivating and appealing to them. They eagerly shared things they had discussed among themselves, yet Jesus waited to answer their question. Instead, he asked them to probe the issues for more detail. We may recognize that Jesus'

15. McHugh, *Listening Life*.

16. Trna et al., "Implementation of Inquiry-Based."

questions were not closed ones that required a "yes" or "no" answer, but he helped the disciples share about their experience and what it meant to them.

"What things?" This is an open-ended, probing question. Jesus probably reinforced their responses, using positive nonverbal communication such as smiling, nodding, and maintaining eye contact. "What things?" This is a clarifying question used for teachers to gain better understanding of a student's ideas, feelings, and thought processes. The question is not for Jesus, but for the disciples to reflect beyond superficial responses.[17] Now it was time for Jesus to teach. Jesus provided them an opportunity to reflect deeply about the events they had shared, but they failed to understand. So, he explained everything clearly and thoroughly. What was the result of his teaching? "Were not our hearts burning within us while he talked with us on the road and opened the Scriptures to us?" (Luke 24:32). The teaching impacted their cognitive as well as social emotional domains.

The last stage of inquiry involves decision-making, which is the essential goal of education and teaching. Now, they fully understood the message of Jesus and immediately made a decision to come back to Jerusalem. They walked seven miles and met the disciples of Jesus there, proclaiming that Jesus has been risen. Teaching mainly consists of two parts: understanding mentally and applying practically. The main teaching activities of the scribes and the Pharisees was simply citing Moses' law. That's why Jesus reprimanded them as "hypocrites" (Matthew 6:5; 7:5; 23:28). They did a good job at memorizing and reciting the law, but not at applying it to their lives. Learning is a changing process where assumptions of old principles and beliefs must be dealt with before accepting new ideas and new learning. In order to accept new knowledge and skills, learners should explore new relationships and regularities through the discovery process. Jesus' questions always inspired his audiences to unlearn old schemata and to explore new ways of thinking and encouraged his listeners to change their perspectives.

Nurturing SEL

The power of education influences students' whole dimensions, including their social emotional domain. Effective teaching impacts students' three domains: 1) mastering knowledge, 2) developing social emotional

17. Carjuzaa and Kellough, *Teaching in the Middle*.

capacities, and 3) strengthening their volitional competence by making the right decisions. Jesus also touched all three dimensions clearly. First, his teaching made them comprehend the Scriptures thoroughly (cognitive domain). Second, his teaching made a positive impact on their hearts, engaging their socioemotional domain. The disciples first looked sad, upon remembering the events surrounding Jesus' death. However, after his teaching, they were invigorated. Their eyes were opened and they elicited how their hearts burned within them. Finally, his teaching made them change their lives and decide their correct action. They immediately returned to Jerusalem and witnessed to what they had seen and experienced.

Gaining Community Actualization

Learning is not just a private personal endeavor, but occurs in community, through the mutually accountable relationships of a learning community in which all students are cared and treated respectfully. Jesus' hospitable teaching made a huge impact on the two disciples as well as the community of disciples who were all excited and encouraged. How do teachers create a hospitable classroom like Jesus did? Burwell and Huyser[18] identify several strategies such as: reading aloud; forming nurturing, caring relationships with students; creating a sense of belonging through welcoming all students into the classroom community by actively forming relationships with one another across perceived differences; designing the syllabi and course together with students.

Once a hospitable community is formed in the classroom, it gradually spreads to all students in the classroom. Leaf explains this as "the law of entanglement."[19] Everything and everyone are linked and all students in the classroom as well as its community affect each other cumulatively.

CONCLUDING REMARKS

Education is a true and powerful intervention from God. That's why Jesus took three years of his earthly ministry for teaching. When he was arrested at Gethsemane, he clearly explained the importance of teaching, saying in Matthew 26:55, "every day I sat in the temple court *teaching*" (italics

---

18. Burwell and Huyser, "Practicing Hospitality," 13.
19. Leaf, *Think, Learn, Succeed*, 110.

added). The power of his teaching was the creation of hospitable spaces for the audience where they freely shared, discussed, and conversed with him. Through this process, his audience changed not only cognitively, but also emotionally and volitionally. "Were not our hearts burning within us while he was talking to us on the road?" (Matthew 24:32). The disciples' journey to Emmaus was gloomy; however, their returning journey to Jerusalem was full of joy and confidence because of Jesus' hospitable teaching.

5

Thriveology for the Emotionally Damaged

Blessed are the meek, for they will inherit the earth.

(MATTHEW 5:5)

A MEEK TEACHER RESTORES A STUDENT WHO HAS STRUGGLED WITH DAMAGED EMOTIONS

THERE IS A STORY about a teacher who was betrayed by a loved one. After the student disowned his teacher three times, he wept bitterly and fell into deep, damaged emotions and feelings with frustration, loneliness, isolation, and rejection, almost losing his hope. However, the teacher came to him, showing compassion for his broken and damaged emotions. The teacher greeted the student and restored him, then reaffirmed his new life mission and vision. The meekness of the teacher made a positive impact on the student, allowing the student to recommend others to be equipped with meekness (1 Peter 3:15). The teacher is Jesus and the student is Peter, in John 21.

Peter was the leader of the twelve disciples. He was the initiator, supreme leader, most vocal follower, and most active personality among them. He even outwardly promised to die for his master (Matthew 26:35). However, in the critical moment where his master was caught by Jewish leaders in the courtyard of the high priest's house, Peter denied his master three times. Furthermore, when his master was hung on the cross, he ran away and hid himself with other disciples, locking the door for fear of the Jewish leaders.

He struggled spiritually, mentally, and emotionally because of how he denied Jesus and abandoned him at the cross. He almost lost faith, confidence, and hope in being the person Jesus wanted him to be. At this crucial point, how did Jesus teach Peter? In this chapter, I will address the strategies and dispositional issues that Jesus demonstrated through which teachers may find applicable points to teach their students who have struggled with damaged emotions and feelings.

JESUS' TEACHING PETER WITH ACCEPTANCE AND ATTUNEMENT

Simon was impetuous and unstable. Although Jesus named him Peter (The Rock), he gave little evidence of stability. Jesus told the disciples about his impending death in Jerusalem, but Peter resisted. When the soldiers tried to arrest Jesus in Gethsemane, Peter drew a sword and cut off Malchus's ear. Though Peter had bragged that he would die for Jesus (John 13:37), he denied being his disciple three times: once to a servant girl, once to a man standing by the courtyard fire, and once to one of the high priest's relatives (John 18:17, 25–27). Even after he met the risen Jesus, he still was in the midst of damaged memories and could not believe it. His enthusiasm and vigorous personality were completely drained. He wanted to escape from reality and he went fishing with other disciples. However, they couldn't catch any fish, even though they worked so hard throughout the whole night. This was about the time they heard a familiar and friendly voice toward them: "Friends, throw your net on the right side of the boat." Perplexed, they obeyed the man's voice and a miracle happened: they caught a large number of fish. John recognized the voice of the person, and said to Peter that it was Jesus. As soon as he heard that, Peter returned to his original personality, being impetuous, plunging into the sea to get to Jesus on the beach.

Jesus was waiting for them, preparing a meal for them. There Peter saw a fire of burning coals. After they ate (I am not sure what mood they were in during the meal. Were they happy to reunite with their master? Did they feel embarrassed?), Jesus initiated a significant conversation with Peter. Jesus called Peter by his real name, Simon. "Simon, son of John, do you love me?" Peter answered, "Yes, Lord. You know that I love you." Jesus used the word for *agape* love here, but Peter answered with the word for *philia* love. The same question and answer continued for the second time. Jesus asked for *agape* love, but Peter answered using *philia* love. *Agape* refers to a godly love, a self-sacrificial, volitional one, while *philia* means brotherly love with affection and affinity. "Do you *agape* me Peter?," which means, "Do you have the highest form of love for me, Peter?" Peter replied, "Yes, I love you Lord; I don't love you with all that I am, but I have the deepest affection for you as my best friend, my closest companion."

However, the third time Jesus changed his own question by adopting the word that Peter used (*philia*). "Peter, do you really have deep affection for me? Are you really my friend?" When Peter heard the same question three times continually, he was hurt (John 21:18). Being hurt is a deep grief, more than just being disheartened. Why was he hurt? There are two reasons for this: first, because Peter realized that he had not yet matured to have *agape* love for Jesus; second, because Jesus took Peter back to the scene of his betrayal. His question reminded Peter of his damaged memories from a couple of days ago where he disowned his master three times (John 18:25–27). Peter remembered that after he had denied Jesus a third time, Jesus had looked at him right in front of the chiefs of the Jews during his trial. Peter had promised to give his life for his master (John 13:37), and yet he violated his most important oath, which leads to deeper spiritual damage. He may have told himself, "I am worthless!"

However, Jesus allowed Peter the opportunity to reaffirm his love three times. He then went on to affirm that Peter would ultimately do what he promised to do, give his life for his Lord. Jesus restored Peter's faith, confidence, and hope with one simple question, "Do you love me, Peter?" "If you are really my friend, feed my lambs." Jesus healed Peter's damaged memories with a simple question. How did Jesus heal Peter's awful memories and damaged emotions? We need to remember two key strategies: acceptance for who he is and contextual attunement.

Acceptance for Who He Is

Jesus accepted Peter for who he is. Although Peter had made several critical mistakes, Jesus never blamed him nor pointed a finger at him. He never said, "Why did you do such a terrible thing?" "How many times will this go on?" Instead of blame shifting, he accepted him as he is. This is a crucial step to heal a person with damaged memories. Jesus gently reminded Peter of true love by asking the question, "Do you love me?"

Peter couldn't answer Jesus with *agape* love. Jesus restored Peter by causing him to squarely face his point of failure, then challenged him to turn his eyes to the mission by leading an inquiry. He never rebuked his wrongdoing nor directly confronted his shame and guilt. Jesus didn't ask Peter to promise not to do wrong again. Rather than pointing out Peter's failure, Jesus reminded Peter of his new role and responsibility by reiterating the same question here: "Do you love me? Then take care of my sheep."

This style of teaching made Peter regain confidence and hope, embracing the *agape* love that allowed him to later lay down his life. Peter's initial failure to recognize the kind of love Jesus asked for points to the challenge that lay in Peter's path to take up the role of the shepherd who dies for his sheep.

Contextual Attunement

Seamands[1] introduces an effective counseling technique, referring to as "the healing of memories," in which the counselor works with a person who has struggled with damaged memories. That's why Jesus prepared the charcoal fire in John 21. The New Testament mentions the charcoal fire only twice (John 18 and 21). Jesus remembered that Peter stood in the courtyard warming himself before a charcoal fire when he denied Jesus three times. After Jesus called Peter and his companions from their fishing, he deliberately asked Peter to stand near a charcoal fire. A damaged emotion/feeling could have resurfaced when Peter saw the charcoal fire. Three times he had denied Jesus and three times he would be asked to affirm his love for him, standing before the fire, where Jesus would heal Peter's painful memories. Complete restoration and healing was made and a new life mission and responsibilities were established.[2]

Yes, this is the miracle of education. Jesus is a master teacher. He accepted Peter and healed him in the same environment where he had experienced failure. He set the charcoal fire and asked the same question three times ("Simon, do you love me?") and gave the same answer three times ("Take care of my sheep"). The contextual attuning looks like a surgical

1. Seamands, *Healing of Memories.*

2. Shepherd, "Do you Love Me?"; Lewis, "Shephard My Sheep"; O'Collins, "Easter Healing"; Stapleton, *Gift of Inner Healing.*

tool through which he restored Peter's broken memories and shame. Not only was Peter healed and forgiven, but also he was reaffirmed with a new mission. The contextual attunement gave Peter a fresh future, through the loving and forgiving presence of the risen Lord.[3]

CARING: HEALING STUDENTS' DAMAGED EMOTIONS AND MEMORIES

Many students in the classrooms struggle with damaged emotions and feelings from their parents, guardians, friends, and the toxic social environments mentioned in chapter 1. They have struggled with the feelings of rejection, shame, anger, guilt, fear, doubt, depression, and despair. These negative emotions and feelings originally occurred in childhood, gradually strengthened by their social environments.[4] When students have been abused or neglected, it can leave them feeling wounded, deprived, and wronged by those they had loved and trusted. If these hurts are not resolved, it continues to affect others and their subsequent relationships.

The good news is that there still remain ample possibilities for these students to be healed and restored. For example, Leaf[5] exposes the switch in students' brains that will enable them to live a happier, healthier, more enjoyable life where they achieve academic as well as life goals. How can we do that? In this section, I will explain how to heal and restore students who have been damaged from negative feelings and emotions to live healthier lives using the CARING process.

Cultivating Connections

What do students who have damaged emotions have in common? Students share a deep sense of unworthiness, a continuous feeling of anxiety, inadequacy, and inferiority, an inner nagging that says, "I am not good. I am a failure. Nobody loves me."[6] Therefore, teachers must make connections with these students using encouraging words, not condemning or punishing ones.

3. Lewis, "Shephard My Sheep."
4. Solomon, *Rejection Syndrome*.
5. Leaf, *Think, Learn, Succeed*.
6. Seamands, *Healing for Damaged Emotions*.

Think about what Jesus did to encourage Peter: "Friends, haven't you any fish?" He still loved Peter even though he had experienced Peter's betrayal. He invited Peter to the breakfast banquet and served the meal. Restoring synchrony is critical to cultivate connections with students who experience damaged feelings. Being in sync means resonating through sounds and movements that connect, which are embedded in the daily sensory rhythms of cooking and cleaning, going to bed and waking up. Being in sync means sharing funny faces and hugs, expressing delight and disapproval at the right movement, tossing back and forth, or singing together.[7]

Affirming Personhood

Remember that Jesus never condemned Peter, but accepted him the way he is. One of the hardest things for damaged people to confront is their shame about the way they behaved during a traumatic episode. They despise themselves for how terrified, dependent, excited, or enraged they felt.[8] Like Peter in John 21, their damaged feelings and emotions rob them of their self-esteem. Therefore, the goal of education for these people is to set up their dignity and value, reestablishing ownership of their body and mind.[9] By affirming each person's personhood, let him/her feel free to know what you know and to feel what you feel without becoming overwhelmed, enraged, ashamed, or collapsed.

How may we affirm personhood for students with damaged emotions and feelings? Wagner[10] suggests three crucial strategies. First, provide a sense of belonging in which the student can feel being loved. This is simply the awareness of being wanted, accepted, cared for, enjoyed, and loved. Second is a sense of worth and value. This is the inner feeling of a student who feels that "I count; I am of value; I have something to offer." Finally help students have a sense of competence, so that they may gain a certain level of confidence that "I can do this task; I can cope with that situation; I am able to meet life's challenges." Through these three strategies, we may teach students who are struggling with damaged emotions and feelings and reestablish their self-worth and confidence.

7. Van der Kolk, *Body Keeps the Score.*
8. Van der Kolk, *Body Keeps the Score*, 13.
9. Van der Kolk, *Body Keeps the Score*, 203.
10. Wagner, *Sensation of Being Somebody*, 32–37.

Restoring Relationships

Jesus calls Peter by his name, Simon, each time he asks a question. He didn't lecture or speak at Peter; rather he gently reminded Peter of the essence of *agape* love, "Do you love me?" Reinstalling love in order to restore relationships is crucial for those who struggle with damaged emotions. Think about students who have struggled with damaged emotions and feelings for a long time. The essence of their trauma is dissociation, which manifests in feeling lost, overwhelmed, abandoned, and disconnected from the world and in seeing themselves as unloved, empty, helpless, trapped, and weighed down.[11]

Jensen[12] identifies several tips that teachers may use to teach effectively, including:

- Give respect to students first, even when they seem least likely to deserve it.

- Share the decision making in class.

- Avoid such directives as "Do this right now!" Instead, maintain expectations while offering choice and soliciting input.

- Avoid demeaning sarcasm.

- Model the process of adult thinking.

- Discipline through positive relationships, not by exerting power or authority. Avoid such negative directives as "Don't be a wise guy!" or "Sit down immediately!" Instead say, "We've got lots to do in class today. When you are ready to learn, please have a seat."

In order to do that, the critical teacher's task in a classroom is to foster reciprocity: truly hearing and being heard, really seeing and being seen by other people. Schools should focus on the importance of fostering safety, predictability, and being known and seen. Teachers can make certain that each child is greeted by name every morning and that teachers make face-to-face contact with each and every one of them.[13]

---

11. Van der Kolk, *Body Keeps the Score*, 121.

12. Jensen, *Teaching with Poverty in Mind*, 21.

13. Van der Kolk, *Body Keeps the Score*.

Initiating Inquiry

After restoring the relationship with students, it is the time to initiate a lesson. As I said in chapter 2 (and I will reiterate this in chapter 11), inquiry is a teacher-led instructional strategy in which the teacher introduces a well-designed dialogue based on each student's needs and assets. Through the inquiry process in John 21, Peter experienced three stages of transformation: enlightening, exposing, and equipping.[14]

First, Jesus made the truth known to Peter through the inquiry process. His genuine relationship with a sinful Peter was revealed with the simple question, "Simon, do you love me?" Jesus revealed a plan that led to reconciliation even though Peter had betrayed him, deep in the valley of despair. Jesus even adopted Peter's terminology to challenge Peter's ability to offer even the *philia* he had professed. Then, Jesus let Peter be exposed to the hidden places of his heart. Jesus kept asking the same question three times, in order for Peter to reflect and check his heart, focusing on desensitizing him to their past, with the expectation that re-exposure to his traumas would reduce emotional outbursts and flashbacks.[15] The inquiry is a way of powerfully probing as a living and active tool to shine into the very depths of the heart. Finally, Peter was equipped with a new mission and life goal through the inquiry process. Jesus allowed Peter to regain the position of apostle, and Peter was now commissioned to feed the Lord's lambs and sheep.

How can we initiate an inquiry with students who have damaged memories and emotions? Teachers may take three stages of inquiry: enlightening, exposing, and equipping. In the first stage, teachers may grab students' attention by focusing on lessons with relevant and insightful material so that students may gain new understandings and discernments. It is a creative means of getting students their needs for the information to come in the lesson.

Second, the exposing stage is used to shine a light into the dark areas (or negative sides) of students' hearts by probing their perspectives and lives. This is a difficult but critical time in which students advance or expand their zone of development. A well-organized question-and-answer session is crucial. Lastly, all lessons should be geared toward leaving a positive

14. I have taken the three-stage concept from Richards and Bredfelt (*Creative Bible Teaching*, 56–59) on the role of the Bible. I think those three roles of the Bible perfectly match the process of inquiry that Jesus took to teach Peter in John 21.

15. Van der Kolk, *Body Keeps the Score.*

impact on students' lives. This is called the equipping stage. Teachers need to organize the lesson carefully so that students take something away at the end of the lesson. Students regain skills, competencies, and a positive attitude so that they confront their problems with a fresh perspective. Careful time management with a planned conclusion is always the most effective approach to teaching. The figure below outlines the process of teaching for students who experience deeply damaged feelings and emotions.

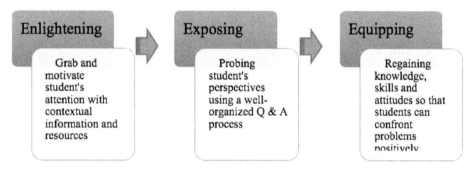

Figure 5.1: Inquiry for Those Who Have Experienced Damaged Emotions and Feelings

Nurturing SEL

Social-emotional support is the most important factor to be considered when teaching students with damaged emotions and feelings. They have been isolated and have suffered with low self-esteem for a long time. Supporting students emotionally with a simple word of encouragement and a kind act is both critical and meaningful. In order to do that, two strategies need to be considered: 1) reciprocity and 2) attunement.

The term *reciprocity* refers to being truly heard and seen by the people around them, feeling that they are held in someone else's mind and heart.[16] In the class, students are allowed to freely express their feelings and behaviors. Secondly, students need to feel that teachers willingly help them with authentic interest and care. Teachers must manifest a similar degree of intensity in their present experience.[17] Not only are they matched emotionally, but teachers must have the same quality of nonverbal expression.

16. Van der Kolk, *Body Keeps the Score*, 79.
17. Hughes, *Attachment-Focused Parenting*, 38.

Palmer asks teachers to create a classroom not only cognitively, but as an emotional space. He points out:

> Teachers must create emotional space in the classroom, space that allows feelings to arise and be dealt with. We often clutter our learning space with obstacles and distractions to evade the emotions that education evokes. If we leave those emotions unattended, we will not be able to clear that space. Fear of feelings and not major barriers to creating the space this sort of teaching requires.[18]

Gaining Community Actualization

Healing one student in a class positively impacts the whole classroom. Jesus' restoration of Peter with the CARING process made a difference to the other disciples, who now all understood the new mission and vision for each of them. This is called "the law of entanglement."[19] Everything and everyone in one organization is linked together. The power of education makes change within one specific student impact more students in the classroom. In order to do that, having a good support network by building caring communities constitutes the most powerful strategy for students who are struggling with damaged emotions. Remember what Jesus has done for Peter. He served meals, warmly greeted, and gently asked questions by reminding him of the love of God to reaffirm his mission. There was no condemnation, reprimand, or criticism. The role of teachers is to provide students physical and emotional safety, including safety from feeling shamed, rebuked, or judged, and to bolster students' courage to tolerate, face, and process the reality of what has happened.

CONCLUDING REMARKS

Education is the only hope for the future of our country and for our children, even though they have struggled with damaged emotions from their parents, friends, and toxic environments. Like Jesus with Peter, a well-organized teaching method and a fully equipped disposition make a difference to our students. In order to do that, schools must provide a safe

18. Palmer, *Promise of Paradox*, 83–84.
19. Leaf, *Think, Learn, Succeed*, 110.

space where all students are seen and known, where they learn to regulate themselves, and where they can fully advance their talents and skills. Even if students are living in a chaotic world, classrooms should be a safe place where students share their emotions in a creative lab where they promote their capacities greatly.

6

Thriveology for the Disabled

Blessed are those who hunger and thirst for righteousness,
for they will be filled.

(MATTHEW 5:6)

THE STORY OF A HOPELESS MAN WHO HAD BEEN DISABLED FOR THIRTY-EIGHT YEARS

WHY DOES TEACHING MATTER? Students in and out of the classroom are children of God equipped with precious knowledge, skill, and competence. The root meaning of "to educate" is "to draw out." The teacher's task is not to fill the student with facts, but to evoke the truth that student holds within to promote hope and optimism. Education is to listen to those who hunger and thirst for righteousness. Our society usually tends to ignore people with disabilities. The power of teaching starts with listening because listening communicates a sense of respect for and an interest in these students' contributions.[1]

John describes a man who had been lying on a pool named Bethesda in John 5:1–15. His only hope was to get into the pool when the water was stirred to be healed. However, because he was disabled, he couldn't move himself to the pool without help. Desperate and anxious, he had tried to do

1. Hammond, *Culturally Responsive Teaching*.

his best to get into the pool for thirty-eight years, but had failed. He was discouraged and resented himself and others, yet nobody took care of him. Only Jesus, who knew his inner motivation that searched for hunger and thirst, took care of him by engaging with him when he was in a deep moment of despair. He saw the man and respectfully asked a critical question: "Do you want to get well?"

How Jesus Taught a Man with Disability

The pool in Jerusalem called Bethesda means "House of Mercy." So many people with disabilities laid there, waiting for an angel to come down at a certain time into the pool and stir up the water. Then, whoever stepped in first would be healed of whatever disease the person had. John 5:6 says, "One who was there had been an invalid for thirty-eight years." The word John uses for "invalid" is the Greek word *asthenia*, which means weakness, infirmity, or diseases. We do not know his name or anything else about him. Based on the information in the Bible, we assume that his physical condition was so severely impaired that he couldn't get into the pool without help from others. Not only his physical condition, but also his social and emotional condition were affected. His friends and family members probably stayed with him at first, but finally left him. Yet, he still stayed, hoping to get into the pool someday.

This person's real issue was not his physical disability, but his emotional trauma and hopelessness. There are three stages that such a person may experience. The first stage is discouragement. People are discouraged when they don't meet their goals or expectations. Dinkmeyer and Dreikurs[2] point out that discouragement is the absence or restriction of courage. A discouraged person has no confidence in their own ability and assumes they have no chance to succeed. They are afraid of what will come, sure that it will not only be dangerous, but hard to bear. Discouraged people perceive themselves to be unable to accomplish their predefined goals because they experienced repeated difficulties and put forth decreasing efforts to learn with each failure.[3] The invalid mentioned in John 5 had tried his best at first to get into the pool; however, he gradually recognized the gap between his expectation and the reality, which lead to a deep level of discouragement.

2. Dinkmeyer and Dreikurs, *Encouraging Children to Learn*, 31.
3. Geraty, "Education and Self-Esteem."

The second stage is learned helplessness. The term *learned helplessness* was originally used as a description of a laboratory animal that fails to escape or avoid shock, but it has gradually been applied to the failure of human beings to pursue, utilize, or acquire adaptive instrumental responses.[4] A discouraged person exercises little voluntary control over his/her environmental events. Think about the situation of the man in John 5. His physical condition prevented him from sitting or standing for a long time and caused him deep, unavoidable frustration. This man's real problem had moved from his physical disability to his emotional hopelessness. Can you imagine his feeling of deep despair and desperation? For thirty-eight years, whenever the water has stirred, this person has tried to do his best to get in the pool, but every time he has failed. Learned helplessness produces three deficits: 1) an undermining of one's motivation to respond, 2) a slowing of one's ability to learn that responding works, and (3) an emotional disturbance, usually depression or anxiety.[5] During the thirty-eight years of his infirmity, he had become accustomed to such a limited lifestyle. He would have had no real hopes or dreams of a future that moved beyond the confines of the portico by the pool.

The last stage is internalized oppression. Learned helplessness had eventually led to this person's belief that he couldn't do something, giving up all opportunities to learn or try new things and hurting his identity.[6] Think about this man's repeating failures for thirty-eight years. He might have blamed himself, which hurt his identity and his worth. He might have internalized the negative social messages about his life, which caused him to lose confidence and identity.[7]

In this situation, how did Jesus teach him? The goal of his teaching was to build hope and optimism.[8] Jesus knew that learned helplessness is not a genetic phenomenon, but an adaptive response to harsh life conditions. Hope and optimism can be learned by all discouraged students who are experiencing trauma and adversity. How did Jesus approach this person? Jesus used three strategies in this case.

First, Jesus fully understood the person's condition. Read John 5:6: "When Jesus saw him lying there and learned that he had been in this

4. Seligman, "Learned Helplessness."

5. Sutherland and Singh, "Learned Helplessness," 171.

6. Becktold, "Brain Based Instruction."

7. Hammond, *Culturally Responsive Teaching*.

8. Jensen, *Teaching with Poverty in Mind*.

condition for a long time." Pay attention to two critical words in this verse, "saw" and "learned." What did Jesus see? Jesus mercifully saw this man's life. Jesus clearly knew that every human being possesses an inherent dignity, meaning, and worth regardless of the person's physical conditions, abled or disabled. What Jesus saw was a unique respect for his life. Being merciful is a critical disposition to possess for effective teachers. In addition, Jesus learned of his psychological condition. This man had been isolated and had no one to help him. He wanted to get into the pool when its waters were stirred, but he had no confidence in that hope. There were so many people around the pool, yet there was no helper to assist this person. Nobody cared for him except for Jesus, who saw this man and sought to actively involve him in what was to happen.

Second, Jesus guided him in unlearning his learned helplessness. His hope had almost died. However, Jesus ignited this person's willingness and enthusiasm, which were hidden in him for a long time, by asking a critical question: "Do you want to get well?" (John 5:6). He didn't teach this person the causes and effects of the diseases or strategies of how to get into the pool first. Jesus awakened his motivation. Of course, he wanted to get well. However, his hope to get well had turned into useless delusions after he had repeatedly failed to get into the pool. In this critical moment, Jesus' question rekindled and bolstered him to remember his hope.

"Do you want to get well?" (John 5:6). This question served to remind him of his identity and his hope. "Do you want to get well?" This was not a command. Jesus gently invited him to open dialogue, through which Jesus helped him reset his life in a different way. This question inspired him to awaken his hope that things would be better in the future.

What was the answer to the question Jesus asked? "Sir, I have no one to help me into the pool when the water is stirred. While I am trying to get in, someone else goes down ahead of me." (John 5:7). The tone of this man reflects frustration. His point is, "Yes, I want to be healed, but I can't. I've tried everything I know and I do, but I lack the ability." However, Jesus recognized that he was willing to be healed. Through his conversation with Jesus, this man realized his situation, which was as dim as his personal aspirations.[9]

Jesus knew this person's situation and inspired him to revive hope. This is the power of education. Finally, Jesus encouraged him to take positive action. John 5:8 says, "Then Jesus said to him, 'Get up! Pick up your

9. Anderson, *Reaching Out and Bringing In*.

mat and walk.'" Jesus asked him to do something to check his willingness before he was made well. This person was now ready to do something after he recovered his mental, emotional, and psychological health. The figure below is a summary of Jesus' teaching to overcome the hopelessness of the person in John 5.

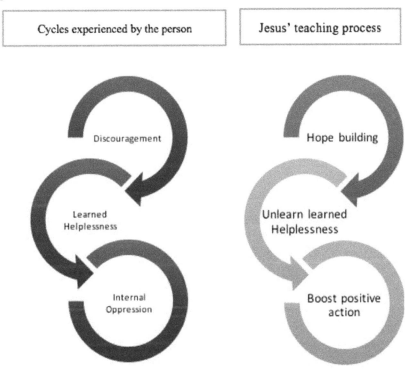

Cycles experienced by the person

Jesus' teaching process

Discouragement

Learned Helplessness

Internal Oppression

Hope building

Unlearn learned Helplessness

Boost positive action

Figure 6.1: Cycles Experienced by the Person in John 5 and Interventions that Jesus Takes

HOPE REGAINED FOR STUDENTS WITH DISABILITIES: CARING PROCESS

Like the person by the Bethesda pool who waited to be carried into the pool, there are many students sitting in the classroom, losing hope and waiting for teachers to come and help them. Students with disabilities have suffered physically as well as socially and emotionally, which causes a lack of confidence and loss of belonging. Like the person in John 5, people with disabilities are neglected and mistreated by more able-bodied members of society. You may get a sense of his loneliness and near hopelessness when the man replied to Jesus with despair, saying, "I have no one to put me into the pool when the water is stirred up" (John 5:7) The good news is that he did not completely give up hope that he would be healed. The main goal of teaching students with disabilities is to instill hope and optimism by unlearning their learned helplessness and internalized oppression. How can teachers do that?

Cultivating Connections with Empathy

Interestingly, meeting the invalid (unfortunately we do not know this person's name) in the pool was not the original purpose of Jesus' visit to Jerusalem. He came to Jerusalem to observe Passover, the Jewish holy day. However, his focus was on the man lying by the pool rather than on the rituals of the festival. Sometimes, teachers may over-prioritize their planned activities and curriculum. However, there may be an off-ramp that can serve as a life-changing moment for a certain student with whom a teacher can make a crucial connection with an opportunity for encouragement.

This person might have met people around the pool for thirty-eight years, yet he didn't get any practical help from any of them. Only Jesus could inspire and reignite his hope. What made Jesus' teaching effective in this case? It was through his connection with the man. Jesus understood this person's situation and prior life clearly. Even though Jesus probably saw many disabled people lying at the pool (John 5:3), his eye was on one person, the invalid, who still didn't give up the hope of being healed. The critical point of connection was made through Jesus' empathy. As the wounded healer, Jesus was fully empathetic with this person's physical as well as emotional pain and suffering because Jesus himself had experienced many adversities since his birth.[10] Jesus took care of him with authentic respect and care, accepting him fully as a complete human being.

Jesus learned that he had been in this condition for a long time (John 5:6). The person had been occupied with fear, anxiety, and frustration for his unsuccessful practices over thirty-eight years, which had led to his helplessness and internalized oppression. When students experience anxiety, frustration, and trauma, their academic performance is interfered with by the stress hormone cortisol, which in turn reduces the amount of working

10. Nouwen, *Wounded Healer*.

memory available to them to do complex tasks.[11] In order to implement effective teaching for students who experience trauma, teachers' attitude and mindset is crucial. When teachers act with empathy, they seek to enter into the world of students with disabilities.[12] Therefore, empathy and attitude are two critical competencies to develop in order to connect with students with disabilities. For example, empathetic teachers show more favorable attitudes towards students with special needs.[13] After interviewing teachers on the topics of the barriers to effective inclusion, Glazzard[14] also identifies that teachers' attitudinal barriers against students with special needs is a significant challenge. Teachers need to embrace the beliefs that all students can learn and can be successful regardless of their physical conditions and/or mental impairment.

Affirming Personhood

The power of Jesus' teaching was that he was comfortable with any group of people. He became a friend of all and taught everyone equally and respectfully, including people who were despised by Jewish leaders, such as prostitutes, tax collectors, Samaritans, and children. Jesus knew that all people are created in God's image and share the same value. Still, we judge others, especially people with disabilities, based on a normative bias, which is an unquestioned worldview that carries the idea that people with disabilities are less than normal.[15] The normative bias leads one to view the world with a dichotomy; have or have not, able or disabled, normal or abnormal, superiority or inferiority, minority or majority. In classrooms, students with different learning needs are considered objects to be filled, to be taken care of, bodies that need help and assistance. However, Jesus connected with this person with authentic respect and care, fully accepting him as a complete human being, not as having a limited capacity. The purpose of education is to actualize all people's potential, which was planted in them by God, through which he intends to build a community of shalom. Salend[16] identifies the hallmarks of effective teaching strategies: 1) it wel-

11. Leaf, *Switch on Your Brain*; Hammond, *Culturally Responsive Teaching*.

12. McHugh, *Listening Life*.

13. Parchomiuk, "Teacher Empathy and Attitudes."

14. Glazzard, "Perceptions of the Barriers."

15. Anderson, *Reaching Out and Bringing In*; Wolterstorff, *Educating for Life*.

16. Salend, *Creating Inclusive Classrooms*.

comes, acknowledges, and celebrates the value of all students by educating them in high-quality, age-appropriate methods; 2) all students are valued as individuals capable of learning and contributing to society; 3) teachers are reflective practitioners who are flexible, responsive, and aware of students' needs; and 4) it involves collaboration among educators, other professionals, students, families, and community agencies.

Restoring Relationships

"I have no one to help me into the pool. . . . When I am trying to get in, someone else goes down ahead of me" (John 5:7). This man was frustrated and angry. He thought that the reason why he hadn't gotten well was because there was nobody to help him. He blamed others for his failure. Yes, he had lost relationships with others, a major problem in his life. Jesus may have been the first person to build an authentic and trustworthy relationship with him, finally allowing this person to be healed. What can teachers learn from this to build trusting relationships with students with disabilities?

First, teachers' attitudes toward and rapport with students are critical factors in order to teach students effectively.[17] As Jesus demonstrates, teachers must host a space where students are encouraged to disarm themselves, to lay aside their pains and frustration, and to listen with attention and care to the voices speaking in their own center.[18] Building a relationship means listening to others by centering the mind, heart, and posture on the other person.[19] In order to do that, teachers need to know students' background and context, including their pain, fear, frustration, and grief.

Second, a teacher's caring relationship with students who are experiencing instability and disability serves as a powerful strategy for them to grow. Caring involves a displacement of interest from the teacher's reality to the reality of students. Therefore, the motivation of the teacher is the welfare, protection, or enhancement of the students.[20] Benard[21] also characterizes caring relationships as ones consisting of compassion, respect, active

17. Carson, "Thirty Years of Stories"; Chickering and Gamson, "Seven Principles."

18. Nouwen, *Reaching Out.*

19. McHugh, *Listening Life.*

20. Nodding, *Caring.*

21. Benard, *Resiliency.*

listening, and high expectations, and identifies caring relationships as one critical strategy to teach students with special needs effectively.

Initiating Inquiry

Education is not simply offering new information or dispensing basic facts into students' minds. Rather, it is drawing out knowledge that students already possess using the question-answer inquiry process. Jesus started the lesson with a question, "Do you want to get well?" Questioning is powerful. There are many reasons why teachers ask questions to students: to clarify concepts, to correct wrong information, to guide thinking patterns, to affirm key information, and to motivate personal thought. Jesus' question was designed to motivate this person to remind him of his situation and identity. This question offered both care and push, challenging him to take more cognitive and behavioral risk and gain confidence. His question was intended to confront the fear and frustration that had inhibited the growth of this man's intellectual and psychological capacity. At this point, the teacher is a warm demander who encourages students to get out of their comfort zone using a well-designed inquiry process in which students use their own learning to accomplish learning goals.

Active listening without criticism was another critical factor of the dialogue between Jesus and the man. "I have no one to help me into the pool . . . " (John 5:7). Jesus did not criticize his lack of confidence, because he knew this man's condition. Jesus allowed him to share his feelings of frustration and anger in the space that Jesus invited him into. Teachers may remember that just staying beside students is itself a powerful action. Sometimes just listening to a student's own breath and the natural sounds of the classroom or environment can help them push aside chatter, become centered, and make space for thought. Teachers need to know the value of silence in classrooms.

Finally, we learn in this case that the powerful result happened after this person was healed. Later, Jesus found him at the temple and warned, "Stop sinning or something worse may happen to you" (John 5:14). One key strategy of trauma-sensitive education is to resist retraumatization.[22] Retraumatization is a conscious or unconscious reminder of past trauma that results in a reexperiencing of the initial trauma event, triggered by a situation, an attitude or expression, or by certain environments of the

22. Hosinger and Brown, "Preparing Trauma-Sensitive Teachers."

original trauma. That's why the purpose of education is not just curing the symptoms, but solving the real problem, by applying what students learned to their life situations. After he was healed and regained his strength, the man learned the truth. Therefore, the inquiry process is not complete in the classroom, but continues to inform students' lives because the purpose of education is not simply understanding knowledge, but transforming students as well as their society by applying what they have learned.

Nurturing SEL

Teachers should remember that teaching is not limited to improving academic skills, but includes promoting students' interpersonal, social and emotional capacities as well.[23] What made Jesus' teaching successful in the case of John 5? Proximity was the key. Over so many years, this person had lost all of his friends and families. He was left alone. Jesus was the first person who talked to him. When students are experiencing trauma and adversity, the first thing that teachers should do is to stay with them and send the message that "You are not alone; we will get through this together." The key point to this story is that "Jesus learned that he had been in this condition for a long time" (John 5:6). Jesus not only stayed with him but also empathized deeply with his condition, his sense of helplessness and frustration. Understanding a student's needs and assets is an important strategy to nurture students' social-emotional skills.

Second, promoting self-esteem in students can improve their ability to advocate for themselves. Students with low self-esteem often make negative statements about themselves that hinder their performance, such as "I can't," "I don't deserve," "I fail." Jesus' strategy to promote this person's self-esteem was twofold: 1) to listen to his pain and frustration with empathy, 2) yet allow him to face challenges with a motivated mindset by asking a question. Here the teacher's role as a warm demander is essential. In order to be an effective warm demander, Bondy and Ross[24] suggest the following strategies:

- Build relationships deliberately.
- Learn about students' cultures.
- Communicate an expectation of success.

23. Parker and Folkman, "Building Resilience in Students."
24. Bondy and Ross, "Teacher as Warm Demander."

- Provide learning supports.
- Support positive behavior.
- Be clear and consistent with expectations.

There are five areas of social and emotional capacities: self-awareness, self-management, social awareness, relationship skills, and responsible decision-making. We do know that the man became more responsible and maintained a more positive relationship with others after he was healed by Jesus. John 5:15 says, "The man went away and told the Jewish leadership that it was Jesus who had made him well." He had been reluctant to share what happened to him, but now he confidently spoke about his life and about Jesus, who healed him. This is the power of social-emotional learning.

Gaining Community Actualization

We do not know how this person changed his community after he was healed. We only know that he confronted the Jewish leaders and clearly explained that Jesus healed him. But I need to address the importance of building an inclusive community where all students are included respectfully regardless of ability or disability. Education is an intentional activity through which students gain knowledge of themselves in relationship to others, including God and other human beings. This kind of relationship is clearly described in Isaiah 11:6, where the lion and the lamb lie together.

This is a typical example of a community of shalom, where everything exists in the order that God created. The term *shalom* refers to wholeness. In the community of shalom, all people and cultures are linked together in unity, contributing to society with their unique qualities and God-given special gifts. Therefore, education is an intentional intervention through which everyone shows love and compassion to each other as well as promotes equality and justice among all people.

CONCLUDING REMARKS

Jesus teaches us that those who hunger and thirst for righteousness are blessed (Matthew 5:6). Righteousness means right relationships with God and with people.[25] In order to live righteously with God and with people, we need

---

25. Hahn, *Matthew.*

to teach students with disabilities with care and empathy. All students have unbounded potential for growth. Teachers should instill absolute respect for human dignity and universal worth in students and so inspire them to fully actualize their potential.

7

Thriveology for the Culturally Marginalized

Blessed are the merciful, for they will be shown mercy.

(MATTHEW 5:7)

A STORY OF A CULTURALLY PREJUDICED PERSON

WE LIVE IN THE age of turmoil and perpetual conflict. America has been skewered socially, racially, ethnically, and spiritually. Everyday our society is filled with horrible news of bullying and victimization on work sites, in classrooms, and even in church sanctuaries. People develop conscious and unconscious preconceptions, stereotyped beliefs, prejudices, and discrimination against groups based on race, sex, religion, culture, and disability. I believe that any kind of prejudice, stereotype, and discrimination is sin because it stands against the biblical truth that all people are created in God's image and likeness. As I mentioned earlier, building a community of shalom is the goal of education, by reconciling each person with the Creator, with fellow humans, and with nature.

While Jesus exercised his earthly ministry, there was much animosity. The nation was divided; Jews and Samaritans severely hated each other and developed negative prejudices against the other. The Jews despised Samaritans, and Samaritans didn't associate with Jews. Jesus clearly understood that evangelism would be possible only after reconciling both groups. That's why Jesus left the command before he ascended to heaven, saying, "you will be my witnesses in Jerusalem, in Judea, in Samaria, and to the ends of the earth" (Acts 1:8). With this in mind, Jesus taught a lawyer with the Parable of the Good Samaritan in John 10.

THE PARABLE OF THE GOOD SAMARITAN

Historically, there has been a severe and long-standing hatred between Jews and Samaritans.[1] Assyria conquered Israel (the Northern Kingdom) in 722 BC, and took most of the Israelites into captivity, bringing foreigners from Mesopotamia and Syria to live in the Northern Kingdom, where they brought their pagan idols to worship them. They eventually came to be called "Samaritans." The people of Judah (the Southern Kingdom), where Jerusalem was destroyed by Babylon in 586 BC, were also carried off into captivity to the Babylonian Empire for seventy years. Then, King Cyrus of Persia, who conquered Babylon, decreed that Jews must return to their home country. These Jews detested the Samaritans, who intermarried and worshipped pagan gods, which led to severe enmity and animosity between Jews and Samaritans. Jews regarded the Samaritans as corrupt and apostate, so they no longer allied with Samaritans.[2] This sets up the background for the Parable of the Good Samaritan (Luke 10:25–37).

Luke explains the setting like this: "On one occasion an expert in the law stood up to test Jesus" (Luke 10:25). The expert's question seems odd because he already knew the law. He would only have been asking the question to boast of his knowledge and look down upon Jesus for his lack of knowledge in the law. "What must I do to inherit eternal life?" To answer his question, Jesus could have directly mentioned the law of Moses. However, Jesus refused to give a straight response, but elicited an answer from the lawyer himself. This is the way of Jesus' teaching. Jesus did not give the right answer; rather he inspired his audience with another question or story. This was quite different from the teaching styles of rabbis, who usually lectured concerning the law, viewing teachers as responsible for depositing knowledge into students. Freire[3] calls this the "banking model" of education.

1. Wood, *Survey of Israel's History*.
2. Smith, *John*.
3. Freire, *Pedagogy of the Oppressed*.

Lee[4] differentiates the teaching style of Jesus with that of Jewish leaders. The table below shows the major differences between the two.

Table 7.1: Comparison the Teaching between Jewish Leaders and Jesus

Criteria	Jewish leaders	Jesus
Purpose of teaching	Dissemination of information; remembering the Law	Teaching disciples to be fully like him (Luke 6:40)
Method of teaching	Transmittal mode of teaching; recitation, memorization, mouth-to-mouth	Active learning with reasoning (listening and questioning); Relationship oriented (heart-to-heart)
Target focused on teaching	Behavioral change by observing customs and laws	Integrating heart and behaviors; changing visible (behaviors) and invisible (heart) areas
Outcomes of teaching	Mastery of content (Laws)	Transform their lives by applying the learning

"Do this and you will live" (Luke 10:28). Jesus knew the purpose of learning. Learning is not completed in the classroom; it should instead be extended to students' lives by applying what they have learned. Knowing something itself is not enough, but it becomes powerful when it changes lives. The power of Jesus' teaching always lies in his emphasis on application. When Jesus forgave an adulterous woman, he said, "Go now and leave your life of sin" (John 8:11).

However, the story headed in a completely different direction when the lawyer asked another question: "Who is my neighbor?" His question derived from Jesus' previous statement, "love your neighbor as yourself." This was the turning point for Jesus, an opportunity to reteach what the term *neighbor* truly means. The lawyer had learned this term only when referring to fellow Jews, based on Leviticus 19:18, where one's neighbor could

4. Lee, "Jesus' Teaching through Discovery."

be cautiously construed as being limited in scope.[5] This narrow-minded understanding of a neighbor exhibits a stereotyped overgeneralization that displays a sort of we/they orientation, a prejudicial perspective and a bias against other racial and cultural groups.[6] This was an opportunity to teach the authentic meaning of the term. A teachable moment is a point in time in a particular place (usually a classroom) when a teacher has the opportunity to deliver a message about a concept or a procedure in such a way that a light goes on for students and they thereafter understand that concept or can carry out that procedure.[7] Effective teachers catch critical moments when students are engaged and interested in learning new knowledge accordingly. To Jesus, this is a critical time for the lawyer to change his narrow mindset and Jewish-centric worldview.

However, Jesus never taught directly, a byproduct of his unique teaching style. Jesus never spoon-fed his students. Rather, he introduced the Parable of the Good Samaritan in this critical moment. In the story, as we may already well know, a man was robbed, beaten, and left by the side of the road. A priest came by but passed to the other side of the road. Think about how the lawyer may have responded to the priest's actions. He might have understood the priest's intentions, thinking that the priest would have become ritually impure if he touched the man, so the priest's actions would be excused. Then, a Levite, a member of the priestly class, came by. He also ignored the wounded man. Hearing this, the lawyer might have been uncomfortable and perhaps a bit angry. But when Jesus introduced a Samaritan as the hero of the story, rather than the priest or Levite, the lawyer was shocked. The shock came from the fact that it was not a Jew but a hated Samaritan who saved the day. The Samaritan even risked his life, transporting the man to an inn in Jewish territory.

At this point, the lawyer might have argued with Jesus, saying, "Teacher, you are wrong. Samaritans never help Jews; they were originally evil, so they are not compassionate to this person. This would never happen." Jesus might have smiled and kept telling the story. After, Jesus asked one final, but piercing question, "Which of these three do you think was a neighbor to the man who fell into the hands of the robbers?" (Luke 10:36). Jesus employed this question to challenge the assumptions of the lawyer, who was confused at this moment. Who is my neighbor? The lawyer had learned

5. Tinker, "Ministries of Mercy."

6. Hoyer and McDaniel, "From Jericho to Jerusalem."

7. Thompson, "Anatomy of a Teachable Moment," 19.

that his neighbors are his fellow Jews, but the concept didn't make sense in his mind.

The lawyer continued thinking and reflecting upon his worldview and finally changed his narrow-minded perspective of whom he regarded as his neighbor. He answered, "The one who had mercy on him" (Luke 10:37). This revelation exposed his transformed perspective, accepting the hated Samaritans as his neighbors. Jesus' powerful teaching through parables transformed perspectives. That's why people were amazed by Jesus' teaching. He did not lecture, explain the origins of the term *neighbor*, or discuss why Samaritans could in fact be his neighbors. All Jesus did was tell a story and ask a critical question. Jesus concluded with a final but impactful statement: "Go and do likewise" (Luke 10:37).

CARING: INVOKING MEEKNESS TO TEACH STUDENTS WHO HAVE BEEN CULTURALLY MARGINALIZED

Classrooms are microcosms of society, a logical place to address cultural and racial prejudice, and prepare students to function in today's diverse society. Prejudice is a negative attitude toward a certain cultural group.[8] Creating a class dynamic that is welcoming and supportive is one of the responsibilities of a teacher. Teachers should not allow any kinds of prejudice in and out of the classroom. How can teachers do this? Based on the story that Jesus taught in John 10, I will address the CARING process used to reduce cultural prejudice.

Cultivating Connections

Can teachers make a positive connection with a student who comes to test the teacher's knowledge and to argue with the teacher to justify himself? Jesus is willing to take a risk by making connections with students like these. Jesus anticipates the arrogant posture of the lawyer who looks down on Jesus by bragging about his expert knowledge in the law. Like Paul said in 1 Corinthians 8:1, "knowledge puffs up but love builds up." Jesus knows that knowledge on its own merely inflates a person up, making oneself arrogant and egoistic. Only self-sacrificial love (mercy), edifies people. Prejudice begins with a lack of love. The only intervention to reduce prejudice is to

---

8. Stangor, "Study of Stereotyping," 2.

demonstrate love and compassion to all human beings unconditionally (John 15:12).

The lawyer finally recognizes the power of mercy, answering "the one who had mercy on him" (Luke 10:37). In fact, Jesus demonstrates mercy to the lawyer, patiently waiting for his responses, organizing his lesson to rebuke his narrow perspective both indirectly and gently. Finally, Jesus asks a critical question that makes him deeply reflect upon his definition of "neighbor."

Jesus connects with the lawyer by relating with him. Jesus did not answer the lawyer's first question, even though he knew the answer. Rather, Jesus allows him to boast of his professional knowledge. This is a powerful instructional strategy for students to engage in learning activities. From now on, the lawyer keenly listens to what Jesus has to say. In order to cultivate connections with students, teachers must first get to know students' contexts, backgrounds, and circumstances. Concrete connections with the life experiences of the students is a critical starting point of successful teaching.

Affirming Personhood

The Bible clearly declares that prejudice and racism are sins. God doesn't want us to live with prejudice nor be separate from other cultures and ethnicities. Hence, education is our intentional response to reconcile all cultures and ethnicities that are discriminated against based on national, racial, and /or cultural grounds. When we show prejudice, we reject the truth of God, a pretty serious accusation, disobeying the plain truth of the Scripture. Education affirms the absolute value, authority, and dignity of individuals and expresses the belief that all are created in the likeness of God.

Teachers need to intentionally reduce any kinds of prejudice and racial hatred against other cultures or ethnicities in and out of the classroom. In order to do that, there are two things that teachers need to do. First, teachers need to develop self-awareness of the ways that their own biases and attitudes influence their instructional decisions. Tanguay, Bhatnagar, Barker, and Many[9] developed a list of checking for a teacher's cultural awareness, which includes:

- Developing cultural and sociolinguistic consciousness;

9. Tanguay et al., "AAA+ Professional Development," 4.

- Assessing funds of knowledge: self-awareness and others' assets;

- Uncovering biases, attitudes;

- Understanding policies affecting teaching English Learners; and

- Including specific topics on cultural, linguistic, and racial diversity.

Secondly, teachers may realize that only when they understand students' cultural background can they design and deliver instruction to meet diverse students' needs. Therefore, teaching methods and procedures should be modified and differentiated based on students' cultural and social contexts. Zeichner[10] has summarized a set of elements for effective teaching for culturally diverse students from extensive literature. Among them, there are several important elements that teachers need to be aware of: 1) teachers have a clear sense of their own ethnic and cultural identities; 2) teachers are personally committed to achieving equity for all students and believe that they are capable of making a difference in their students' learning; 3) scaffolding is provided by teachers that links the academically challenging and inclusive curriculum to the cultural resources that students bring to school; 4) teachers explicitly teach students the culture of the school and seek to maintain students' sense of ethnic-cultural pride and identity; and 5) parents and community members are encouraged to become involved in students' education and are given a significant voice in making important school decisions.

Restoring Relationships

Connecting to students' cultural and linguistic context always matters in order to build a safe and healthy classroom environment. Jesus started his conversation with the lawyer by addressing the Jewish law with which the lawyer was familiar. Similarly, teachers need to identify students' cultural assets and needs. This is the key to culturally relevant teaching. It is to use cultural knowledge as a scaffold to connect what the students already know to new concepts and content in order to promote effective processing.[11] To implement effective culturally relevant teaching, there are four components that teachers need to think about seriously: awareness, information

10. Zeichner, *Educating Teachers*, 23.
11. Hammond, *Culturally Responsive Teaching*.

processing, community building, and learning partnership. The feature below is the summary of a well-designed culturally relevant teaching model.[12]

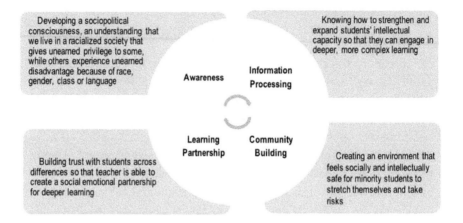

Figure 7.1: Components of Culturally Responsive Teaching

Another important skill that teachers may use to build a positive relationship with students is active listening. The lawyer was not seeking answers from Jesus, but an opportunity to brag about his knowledge. However, Jesus had an acute ability to detect underlying needs, and so probed to the deeper levels of his true desire. Jesus returned the lawyer's question with another question, and in doing so forced the lawyer to reveal his intentions.[13]

Initiating Inquiry

Why did Jesus introduce the story of the Good Samaritan to the prejudiced lawyer? Because the story gave the lawyer an opportunity to create an awareness and critical understanding of his own prejudice. Prejudice refers to one's negative judgement toward a certain culture or a certain group of people. Usually it starts and strengthens by differentiating in-group and out-group boundaries. In-group members are perceived as more desirable and normal, thus deserving to be treated with the warmth and regard owed to them, while out-group members are perceived as more likely to have

12. Hammond, *Culturally* Responsive *Teaching*, 18–20.

13. McHugh, *Listening Life*.

negative connotations, thus susceptible of the stereotypical and negative attitudes and behavior appropriate in relation to such a person.[14]

Delgado[15] proves that stories provide insights into structural preju- dice, shedding light on the need to invoke societal change, thereby em- powering the audience to transform society. Prejudice can be reduced and corrected after engaging a well-planned dialogue, discussion, and/or reflec- tive critical thinking activity.[16] Using the story, Jesus let him examine the criteria or guidelines that he had set in making prejudiced judgements.

Jesus initiated three stages of the inquiry process: 1) unlearning (for- getting the narrow understanding of neighborhood); 2) learning (adopting the new way of neighborhood); and 3) relearning (stabilizing new learn- ing to his future life) stages. In fact, the three-stage change movement was introduced originally by Lewin.[17] In the unlearning stage, Jesus challenged him by framing a question that brought a degree of disequilibrium (cogni- tive dissonance). It involves dismantling old practices and beliefs. It is a process of being influenced by new understandings. On the topic of un- learning, Mark Bonchek writes:

> Unlearning is not about forgetting. It's about the ability to choose an alternative mental model or paradigm. When we learn, we add new skills or knowledge to what we already know. When we unlearn, we step outside the mental model in order to choose a different one.[18]

In order to confront traditional teachings, Jesus communicated a story, parable, or allegory. This made his audience reflect on their perspec- tives and worldviews, beliefs learned from their forefathers or traditional wisdom. His hidden intention of sharing the story of the Good Samaritan was to convict the lawyer to part with his traditional thoughts. Can you imagine the confusion of the lawyer when he listened to the story? He was most likely baffled and perplexed, because the story was not what he ex- pected. After Jesus told the story of the priest who neglected to care for the wounded man and passed by on the other side, he asked "Was this man a

14. Philip, "Jesus and the Reduction"; Pettigrew, "Intergroup Contact"; Devine and Monteith, "Role of Discrepancy-Associated Affect"; Rothbart et al., "Stereotyping and Sampling Biases"; Allport, *Nature of Prejudice.*

15. Delgado, "Storytelling for Oppositionists."

16. Lipman, "Critical Thinking."

17. Lewin, "Group Decisions and Social Change."

18. Bonchek, "Why the Problem."

neighbor?" Then the Levite ignored the man and passed by on the other side. Jesus asked, "Was this man a neighbor?" From the lawyer's perspective, his initial question might have been whether the man was an Israelite or not. Jesus' intentional emphasis away from the man's ethnicity was absolutely essential to the situation he establishes and what transpires thereafter. After Jesus introduced a Samaritan as the hero of the story, the worldview of the lawyer was seriously undermined.

This is called constructive struggling, in which students engage with challenging problems and thought-provoking tasks that require deep reflective thinking. Prejudice can't be reduced through coercion or psychological manipulation, but through rational persuasion via critical thinking processes.[19] Throughout his reflective thinking process, the lawyer achieved a deeper level of understanding the concept of neighbor. This is the second stage, learning. "Which of these three do you think was a neighbor to the man who fell into the hands of robbers?" The lawyer sparked a paradigm shift. He answered, "The one who had mercy on him" (Luke 10:36–37). Jesus didn't directly point to the neighbors of Jews. While engaging in discourse, the lawyer gained new insight and spiritual discernment.

The lawyer learned that his neighbor could be anyone who helps him regardless of custom, tradition, or nationality. Jesus began to make a fundamental transition from the facts of this particular case to the level of general principle, a principle which represents a major divergence from the Mosaic law (group-oriented ethic) to drastically rework the concept of neighbor itself (a universal principle).[20] The learning seemed effectively and successfully complete. However, Jesus went one step further, which is a marker of his teaching, asking him to apply what he had learned to his life: "Go and do likewise." This is the relearning stage. In this conclusion to the conversation, Jesus was really formulating a new principle altogether: act as a neighbor to people in need.

Nurturing SEL

"The one who had mercy on him." Jesus emphasized mercy in order to reduce prejudicial perspectives and attitudes. Prejudice reduction needs a critical reflection process where people deeply review their perspective, prejudice, and bias using a case or story or cooperative learning activities.

19. Siegel, *Educating Reason.*
20. Philip, "Jesus and the Reduction."

Dovidio and others[21] identify four effective interventions to reduce prejudice: multicultural education, intergroup dialogue, cooperative learning, and values-based education. Here, I want to emphasize the importance of values-based education, where teachers strengthen students' social-emotional capacities such as self-awareness, self-management, social awareness, relationship skills, and responsible decision-making. Why? Because prejudice is a debris of a negative attitude and emotional responses toward a certain cultural group.[22]

The Bible clearly recognizes the power of mercy to build positive relationships among individuals and between two groups. For example, merciful people help those who are hurting (James 2:15–17). Merciful people are patient with difficult people (1 Thessalonians 5:14–15) and kind to their enemies (Luke 6:35–36), and they care for the lost (John 3:16–17). Mercy means to suffer with those who are wounded, to fully enter the situation of the other, sharing in whatever comes.[23] Therefore, mercy is an action, just as Jesus explains in the story of the Good Samaritan, who demonstrates taking care of a wounded person. At the heart of the Good Samaritan parable is mercy toward one who suffers injustice and violence.

That's why culturally responsive teaching serves as an education for justice. It develops students into future democratic citizens by eliminating and reducing any possible prejudice, bias, and hatred against any social-cultural groups. In order to do that, teachers need to equip students with cooperative and collaboration skills among diverse cultural groups and social-emotional competencies such as respect, value, and appreciation for other cultures throughout the curriculum.

Gaining Community Actualization

Education in a pluralistic democratic society should help students to gain the content, attitudes, and skills needed to know reflectively, to care deeply, and to act thoughtfully. As I mentioned earlier, the purpose of education is to build a community of shalom where all students' gifts, talents, and other capacities from God are fully actualized. Educators should build a safe and healthy classroom, not allowing any prejudice or bias to be practiced in the classroom.

21. Dovidio et al., "From Intervention to Outcome."
22. Stangor, "Study of Stereotyping."
23. Brown, *Unexpected News.*

Pang[24] identifies several types of teachers in a school; among them two types are noteworthy: the social action teacher and the caring-centered multiculturalist teacher. The goal of the social action teacher is for all people and cultures to experience equality and justice. The caring-centered teacher's goal is valuing and building a pluralistic society based on compassion, justice, and freedom. Hence, the classroom should be the place where one pursues wholeness by promoting unity and peace among different people. In order to accomplish this, Banks[25] suggests taking the social action approach in teaching, which requires students to make decisions and take action related to the concepts, issues, or problems being studied in the class. The major goals of instruction from this perspective are to educate students for social criticism and social change and to teach them decision-making skills that lead to those ends.

CONCLUDING REMARKS

Equality and equity are two guideposts that Jesus utilized to accomplish social justice. He treated all people equally and respectfully, but at the same time he engaged differently based on each person's specific context and background. Schools and classrooms should be the places where one practices social justice, where all students have equal access to resources and receive equitable treatment regardless of their race, gender, religion, or disability. Social justice is not an add-on for classrooms, but must penetrate through all school curriculums. Like Jesus welcomed sinners, women, immigrants, the disabled, the poor, and children into his circle of fellowship, teachers must embrace and include all students in their classrooms.

24. Pang, *Multicultural Education*.
25. J. Banks and C. Banks, *Multicultural Education*.

8

Thriveology for the Doubting Student

Blessed are the pure in heart, for they will see God.

(MATTHEW 5:8)

THOMAS: THE PERSON WHO IS PURE IN HEART

THOMAS, ONE OF TWELE disciples of Jesus who was also called Didymus (the Greek equivalent of the Hebrew name), was a man who was slow to believe and subject to despondency. He had an ISTJ (introverted, sensing, thinking, and judging) personality, according to the Meyers-Briggs personality indicator. The archetypal image of the ISTJ is an investigator and realist,[1] one who calculates situations carefully, focuses on cold hard facts, and sees things error first. This type of personality usually asks questions before acting, not pretending to understand that which to them is fraught with mystery. This type asks for rationale and evidence for why someone does something.

We get to know Thomas's personality more clearly throughout the Bible. For example, Jesus comforted his disciples by stating that he was going to prepare a place for them, and that they knew the way to the place where he was going. However, Thomas, a very sensing and data-driven personality, couldn't understand this. He wanted clear and detailed directions,

---

1. Yount, *Created to Learn.*

a road map for how to get there. So he proclaimed, "Lord we don't know where you are going, so how can we know the way?" (John 14:5). This, however, was not total disbelief or mistrust; it stood as a simple and pure question, asking for specific steps into the unseen future, an eager inquiry into how this step was to be taken.

Thomas's skeptical character culminated when he missed seeing the risen Jesus when Jesus had appeared to the disciples (John 20:24). Thomas heard that the others had seen Jesus, yet he couldn't believe it and exclaimed, "Unless I see the nail marks in his hands and put my finger where the nails were. And put my hand into his side, I will not believe it" (John 20:25). Although this comment has earned him the label "Doubting Thomas," his reaction seems to be reasonable, considering his character and temperament. As a sensing personality, he wanted evidence to believe in the resurrection of his master. He refused to believe what his colleagues' said without tangible evidence for himself. His doubt was not the denial or rejection of Jesus' resurrection, but reservation until he found evidence. When Thomas saw Jesus, his resolute skepticism vanished, as he accepted and worshipped him.

Thomas was an honest doubter, a pure skeptic who eagerly wanted to find evidence of a certain issue. Nevertheless, he was loyal to his master and full of ardent love for Jesus. Thomas was a man of incredible fidelity and courage. There are many stories that praise his loyalty and love for Jesus. For example, when Jesus noticed that Lazarus was sick in Bethany, he told the disciples to go there from Jerusalem. Yet, some disciples opposed his plan because people there might kill Jesus. At this time, Thomas raised his voice, saying, "Let us also go, that we may die with him" (John 11:16). Who can say that Thomas is a pitiful doubter? Though doubt and skepticism surround him, he nevertheless presented his faith by making a brave decision. His love for Jesus was shown in his speech when Jesus was determined to face the dangers that awaited him in Judea on his journey to Bethany.

Thomas's life story gives us many lessons that we may take into the classroom. First, learning is not passively accepting or following predefined facts that authority figures have already described. Instead, to learn is to deeply reflect, think, and ponder the premise and principles, in search for logic and scientific proof.[2] If a student doesn't understand something, let them speak up, rather than suppress their perspective. In fact, there are many students in the classroom who may have different personality types,

2. Fagin, "Doubter Gives Lessons."

who are a bit vociferous, asking for evidence and data like Thomas. How does a teacher respond to their unique needs? In this chapter, I will address effective strategies that Jesus took to teach Thomas and how to apply his strategies in a classroom setting.

JESUS' SCAFFOLDING STRATEGY TO TEACH A SKEPTIC

"Unless I see and unless I put my fingers into his side . . . " This is not an atheist's plea or a doubter's excuse, but a strong desire to search for the truth. This attitude should not be rejected, but should be recognized and praised. This kind of attitude appealed to Jesus. That's why Jesus' second visit to his disciples served a special purpose: to show his hands and side to Thomas. Jesus never blamed him or criticized Thomas for being a doubter; instead he gently told Thomas, "Put your finger here; see my hands. Reach out your hand and put it into my side. Stop doubting and believe" (John 20:27). Thomas reminds us that faith is not simply an assent to doctrines, creeds, and/or propositions that are set up by others.[3] Did Thomas put his fingers into the side of Jesus? No. As soon as Thomas was granted his wish to see Jesus, his doubt and skepticism faded. Jesus did not rebuke him for his slowness of heart to believe, nor blame him for his lack of faith, but rather granted him just what it is that he needed.

Pure doubt from our students should be seen positively in class in order to aid their quest for the truth. Because of his doubt, Thomas could stand on a firm foundation of faith throughout his remaining life. Jesus positively responded to Thomas's doubt and skepticism, showing him his wounds and telling him to see and to touch. He saw, but he did not touch. He didn't need to. As soon as he saw Jesus, he proclaimed "My Lord and my God" and he worshipped him. His seeing gave way, not just to belief, but to worship. Jesus taught, "Blessed are the pure in heart, for they shall see God" (Matthew 5:8).

How did Jesus teach Thomas? He used two critical strategies to change Thomas's skepticism to commitment. First, Jesus knew his student by name. Jesus had known the personality of Thomas during his three years of public ministry. He fully grasped Thomas's needs and assets. Thomas was a man whose heart is pure and honest, always focusing on facts and data, not depending on intuition and the abstract. Being a skeptic is not being

---

3. Fagin, "Doubter Gives Lessons."

distrustful. Jesus was not offended by Thomas; he simply showed him the wounds and marks on his body.

Second, Jesus accepted his pure skepticism. Jesus never condemned a person's skepticism; he instead held it as another way to pursue the truth. The same thing happened with John the Baptist, who was prisoned by Herod Antipas and faced death. Though he may have had his doubts about Jesus, Jesus had deep respect for him. John sent his disciples to Jesus to ask a question: "Are you the one who is to come, or shall we look for another?" (Matthew 11:3). Even with John's skeptical attitude, Jesus esteemed him by saying that John is great in this world. He never condemned or rebuked John's doubt. Jesus affirmed his pure skepticism and answered him accordingly.

Lastly, Jesus used a humble scaffolding strategy. The power of his intervention was that Jesus came to Thomas, not the other way around. Being a vulnerable teacher, Jesus lowered himself down to Thomas's level, showing the shameful marks on his body. He didn't lecture Thomas. He never humiliated him. Without saying any words, he approached Thomas and said, "Put your finger here; see my hands. Reach out your hand and put it into my side. Stop doubting and believe" (John 20:27). Yes, Jesus may have been challenged by Thomas's doubt, but he didn't condemn him for his lack of faith or pessimism. Instead, he came down to Thomas's level, allowing him to overcome his doubt and uncertainty with compassion and acceptance.

God values our pure skepticism. Acts 17:11 says, "Now the Berean Jews were of more noble character than those in Thessalonica, for they received the message with great eagerness and *examined the Scriptures* every day to see if what Paul said was true." Paul also recommends in 1 Thessalonians 5:20-22, "Do not treat prophecies with contempt *but test them all*; hold on to what is good, reject every kind of evil" (italics added).

THE POWER OF PURE DOUBT AND HEALTHY SKEPTICISM[4]

Sadly, current teaching practices do not value student doubt or skepticism in the classroom. Students are encouraged to get higher scores on

---

4. Confusion exists about the terms "doubt" and "skepticism." Usually "doubt" refers to conflicting opinions or evidence for a specific issue or phenomena, while "skepticism" means to act upon that doubt or apply that to a specific area. In this article, I used both

standardized tests, which emphasize low levels of competencies, such as memorizing small facts and understanding relationships between two concepts. Influenced by behaviorism, knowledge is chopped into pieces and fed to students. Students are required to mindlessly accept knowledge as an unconditional form without deeply reflecting or thinking critically.[5] Teachers may value students' critical and creative thinking skills, yet most teaching methods are conducted via teacher-centered models. Students' doubtful and skeptical attitudes should be valued in and out of the classroom, because doubt and skepticism can make the learning more authentic and meaningful.

Doubt, Skepticism: A Search for the Truth

Doubt has been defined as an "inquiry into routine and habitual perceptions and assumptions that are generally conceived as appropriate within some social system of values and beliefs.[6]" Chandler[7] differentiates it two kinds of doubt: a small, case-specific doubt and a large, generic doubt. The former explores methodological faults or logical contradictions with various arguments, while the latter provokes more radical and far-reaching epistemological questions, calling for fundamental inquiry.

Mole[8] identifies doubt or skepticism as holding the same capacity as critical thinking skills, which are prerequisites to being informed, responsible citizens. In fact, critical thinking skills are one of the twenty-first-century critical skills.[9] Critical thinking refers to:

- Revisit, review and reconstruct patterns of beliefs based on new evidence.

- Evaluate evidence for claims and beliefs.

terms (pure doubt and healthy skepticism) interchangeably, referring to critical thinking skills which relates to our attitude or perspective in pursuing the truth which we may withhold until sufficient evidence would be provided. The reason I use the adjectives "pure" and "healthy" is to engage the critical thinking skill through which people engage with new tasks or environments.

5. Langer, *Power of Mindful Learning*.

6. Schechter, "Doubt, Doubting," 3.

7. Chandler, *Othello Effect*.

8. Mole, "Skepticism in the Classroom."

9. See Greenstein, *Assessing 21st Century Skills*; Robinson-Zanartu et al., *Teaching 21st Century Skills*.

- Analyze assumptions and biases.

- Attend to contradictions and ambiguities.

- Recognize unstated assumptions.[10]

Therefore, doubt and skepticism actually describe a search for the truth. The word "skepticism" comes from the Greek *skeptikos*, which means "to reflect, look around, or inquire." Being a skeptic means to think critically, through which people search for the truth and reach their academic as well as professional goals. The power of education is to empower students to develop a personal position through the problem-solving process, through which students clear the possible biases and prejudices that are inherently problematic or that students must abandon.[11] In a classroom, when students think critically, they raise questions, gather relevant information, seek evidence, suspend judgement while considering a variety of possibilities, hypothesize and test out those hypotheses, analyze, and synthesize.[12]

What are the benefits of doubt and skeptical thinking? How does it contribute to learning? First, doubt and skepticism do not invoke pointless frustration or a reckless challenge, but involve constructive struggle and creative conflict, which advances our learning process to be more comprehensive and authentic. Traditionally doubt and skepticism are considered taboo, ineffective, and unproductive. However, they corrects each person's biases and prejudices about nature and issues to solve a given problem. Doubt and skepticism make students reach full cognitive freedom from the confinement of already existing opinions. Students may scrutinize and analyze every statement, throughout the continuous inquiry into the deeply rooted constructs of every perspective.[13] Students distance themselves from their previous experience in order to gain new insight about their life. Therefore, we need to acknowledge that doubt and skepticism are a productive and essential process for human growth. Students have a chance to construct their own meaning, rather than being spoon-fed into submission via one-way transmission of content.[14]

---

10. Greenstein, *Assessing 21st Century Skills*, 24–25.

11. Wright, "Truth, but Not Yet."

12. Robinson-Zanartu et al., *Teaching 21st Century Skills*, 3.

13. Schechter, "Doubt, Doubting."

14. Wright, "Truth, but Not Yet."

Teachers use methods to inspire students' pure doubt and healthy skepticism such as thinking backward, using a zero-based perspective, posing multiple questions, and outside-box thinking so that students see events and phenomena from different angles. Freire[15] calls this process "decoding." It is the critical unveiling process of the codified and objectified situation through attentive, reflective, and interpretive reading of the particular theme. By distancing from their actual experience, students will create a worldview and perspective that leads the new world and reality through the decoding process.

Secondly, doubt and skepticism make learning more enthusiastic and meaningful. It is an ongoing inquiry process through which to find the truth. This is a dynamic procedure between action and reaction working together to offer praxis so that it transforms social reality through ongoing action and critical reflection. Piaget[16] explains the learning process with the disequilibrium theory. When people come across ideas that conflict with their existing schema, disequilibrium occurs and it can be overcome by accepting a new idea or new knowledge. Teachers need to pose disequilibrium intentionally, through which students may be confused for a time being, yet challenged in the long run. Yes, disequilibrium is a strong motivator to learn. It helps students come closer to realizing their potential.[17] Proving learning opportunities through healthy doubt and skepticism is an essential strategy in order for students to temper any reverence for authority with a sense of critical awareness.[18]

Strategies to Boost Students' Doubt and Skepticism

Learning is a changing process in which assumptions of old principles and beliefs must be dealt with by challenging them with new ideas and innovative perspectives. How do teachers boost students' doubt and skeptic capacity within their teaching? First, teachers need to initiate a well-organized dialogue with students. One frequently mentioned dialectic process is the three stages of inquiry, including the thesis, the antithesis, and the synthesis. This process is commonly referred to as the Hegelian dialectic,[19] which

15. Freire, *Pedagogy of the Oppressed.*

16. Piaget, *Equilibrium of Cognitive Structure.*

17. Langer, *Power of Mindful Learning.*

18. Giroux, "Rethinking Education."

19. Schnitker and Emmons, "Hegel's Thesis-Antithesis-Synthesis Model."

includes a beginning proposition, called a thesis; a negation of that thesis, called the antithesis; and a synthesis whereby the two conflicting ideas are reconciled to form a new proposition.

Kurt Lewin[20] also formulates his seminal theory of organizational change using three stages of change (unfreeze, change, refreeze). Among them, the first stage is critically important to lead to organizational change. The unfreeze means the power of pure skepticism and healthy doubt in which people need to distance themselves from old, outdated, biased information and habits. Without effective unfreezing strategies, effective change is not possible. The unfreezing spirit shares the same connotation with Thomas's "unless I . . . " attitude. Rather than merely seeking stability, a student's doubts and skepticism is highly regarded. What are effective unfreezing strategies? Whitin and Whitin[21] identify three strategies supporting students who are skeptics (in math class): 1) examining knowledge in context, 2) challenging the assumptions of models, and 3) exposing the limitations of statistical information. Teachers may embrace many productive strategies to implement the unfreezing, healthy doubting spirit, such as allowing multiple perspectives, opposing ideas, and contradictory perspectives. Teachers need to intentionally facilitate creative conflicts while they are teaching.

Teachers may welcome creative conflict, not because we are angry or hostile, but because conflict is required to correct our biases and prejudices about the nature of great things.[22] They may recognize the value of doubt and pure skepticism, encouraging students to think backwards, with a zero-based perspective, fostering curiosity. Teachers need to understand that conflict can be a positive learning experience through which they lead students to engage and challenge problems that call for more than a superficial application of a rote procedure. Unfortunately, our educational system has failed to teach these skills to our students. Through effective doubt and skeptical processes and unfreezing strategies, we can overcome mystical and irrational phenomena and dogmatic arguments.

20. Lewin, "Group Decisions."

21. Whitin and Whitin, "Learning Is Born of Doubting," 124.

22. Palmer, *Courage to Teach*, 110.

PROMOTING STUDENTS' PURE SKEPTICISM
THROUGH THE CARING PROCESS

There are many students sitting in the classroom like Thomas, who may frequently interfere with class, requiring evidence, facts, and detailed resources. However, teachers mostly ignore their concerns and may even treat them rudely. Teachers need to encourage their questions and perspectives raised during class, not negate this powerful process of learning. How can teachers steward healthy skepticism in the classroom? How can teachers effectively educate those students? In this section, I will address possible interventions through the CARING process.

Cultivating Connections

Then he said to Thomas, "Put your finger here, see my hands. Reach out your hand and put it into my side. Stop doubting and believe" (John 20:27). Jesus cultivated his relationship with Thomas, who was doubting the resurrection of Jesus, in a unique way. First, Jesus came to the home where was Thomas staying. He visited his student's community to make connections. Second, he showed his wounds, the marks where Roman soldiers drove nails into his hands and where his side was pierced with a spear. He shows His vulnerable body, a symbol of persecution, an emblem of pain and shame without hindrance. He is authentic and real. Why? This critical moment of teaching cleared Thomas's doubt and skepticism. Connecting with students who may make trouble is not easy, yet this can become an essential moment for students to learn important lessons.

Yes, education never happens in a vacuum. Effective teaching can be held at any place, at any time, with any topic and resource. For the same reason, teachers can bolster students' pure and healthy skepticism at any time and place.

Affirming Personhood

No matter what, teachers need to show respect to all students regardless of their individual or cultural differences. A teacher should be a success coach regardless of what conditions and situations each student may be confronting. Teachers should be relational mentors who always encourage and inspire their students, honoring them, showing consideration toward them, being concerned about them, appreciating them, relating to them, admiring their strengths, and caring for them. We know that students are experiencing persistently high levels of stress and trauma, and stress can be buffered by the presence of a trusted and calm adult (teacher). That's why the most powerful attribute a teacher can attain is respect for students.[23] In order to do that, teachers need to build a culture of psychological safety in the classroom for students to speak freely and to experience learning mistakes. Bowman posits:

> Mitigating fear in educational settings begins with modeling for students the importance of being open-minded, non-defensive, and intellectually curious in discussing potentially sensitive topics. In a culture of psychological safety, teachers as enablers reassuringly invite challenges to their own views and beliefs and acknowledge and affirm constructive feedback.[24]

Restoring Relationships

After cultivating connections, teachers open the space where they create a positive, interconnected learning environment and where students feel at home and share their concerns and issues freely. Fostering trustworthiness and transparency through connection and communication among students matters always. Teachers should create an atmosphere that promotes and strengthens the relationship or interaction between students and teachers and students with students.[25] Creating and maintaining trust can mitigate the adverse effects of uncertainty and help students find meaning and connection in the classroom. Accepting their ideas and perspectives without blaming and rebuking would make students be more participative in the class. So, students need to feel safe to ask questions.

Initiating Inquiry

Doubt is necessary for all forms of knowledge. Without doubt, there is no inquiry. Moneyhun[26] proposes steps to reasoned inquiry in which students

23. Tomlinson, "One to Grow On."
24. Bowman, "New Story about Teaching," 115.
25. Shanmugavelu, "Inquiry Method."
26. Moneyhun, "Believing, Doubting, Deciding, Acting," 56.

take a systematic stage. Therefore, a well-organized inquiry process should be implemented by teachers for students who may have doubt and skepticism. By taking those four stages of inquiry, students may follow a process of accepting an idea wholeheartedly, then rejecting it no matter how attractive, then choosing what to believe (especially if it wasn't simple acceptance or rejection), and finally applying their clarified belief to a situation requiring action. The table below is the summary of steps to reasoned inquiry. Meaningful discussions emerging from student doubt take multiple forms, which promote different academic purposes.

Table 8.1: Steps to Reasoned Inquiry[27]

Steps	Action verbs to conceptualize	Ways of reasoning
Believing	Believe, accept, summarize or paraphrase, find strengths, understand, tell "what it does"	Idea can be made to fit into a coherent, broader system of ideas; idea confirms personal ideas; idea is supported by proof that is convincing to a person
Doubting	Doubt, reject, state objections, find weaknesses, criticize, tell "what it fails to do"	Idea can't be made to fit into a coherent, broader system of ideas; idea conflicts with the personal experience; idea is not supported by proof that is convincing to a person
Deciding	Decide, choose, weigh ideas, draw conclusions, theorize, tell "what I think"	Idea is useful to creating a system of ideas important to a person; idea clarifies the personal experience; Idea changes, is refined, as a person provides new support

27. Moneyhun, "Believing, Doubting, Deciding, Acting," 56–57.

Acting	Extend, apply, use ideas, act, practice, tell "how it matters"	Idea can be made to fit into real-life contexts not considered by the person; idea tells how to act, treat others, and live; idea is given new life by its use in the world

Students may share what they believe in the first stage (believing). Each student may present his or her adoption and argument for one selected point of view. They may show evidence why they believe a certain idea, ideology, or phenomenon. Then, they may change perspective, see the other side or something they missed or ignored. Teachers have their students work with ill-formed problems or phenomena that are taken for granted in which students unpack, uncover, and decode hidden meaning, unknown facts, and even biases and prejudices. The second stage (doubting) is a key part of the whole process. Doubting the validity of things that have been taken for granted would be a foundational building block for this stage, even if this is not always easy. In-depth data gathering and analyzing, discussing and reflecting on the issue with each other, and reading and searching and interpreting appropriate sources are highly recommended in this stage. Teachers may appreciate multiple perspectives to understand that information can change in different contexts.[28] They also encourage different interpretations of ideas so that not all students give the same answer. Therefore, the teacher may be prepared to listen to and accept different responses from students to a problem.[29] After analyzing all data and comparing the pros and cons of the issue, students may make a final decision (deciding). Lastly, they apply what they decided to their lives (acting).

Inquiry is a teacher-centered dialogue process. Teachers play a key role in setting up the conditions that allow the skeptical attitude to flourish. Whitin and Whitin emphasize the role of teachers to boost students' skeptical stance as explained below:

> First, teachers can encourage knowledge by posing critical questions: how did you come to this conclusion? How else could we interpret this issue? What information is not revealed? What claims can we not make? What new questions do we now have?

28. Whitin and Whitin, "Learning Is Born of Doubting."
29. Shanmugavelu, *Inquiry Method.*

These questions hone the edges of a skeptical mind. Secondly; teachers can capitalize on anomalies when they arise, for instance, by asking: Why might it make sense to feed birds a high-fat diet? Valuing and examining surprise is an essential characteristic of a skeptical attitude themselves by giving alternative interpretations and pointing out contradictory information. In this way, a skeptical stance is not reduced to a separate skill, or limited to a single subject or time frame, rather it becomes an ever-present filter for taking in the world.[30]

Nurturing SEL

Even though doubt and skepticism lead to a higher level of understanding, sometimes they may cause students to lack motivation. Critical thinking skills depend heavily on intrinsic rather than extrinsic motivation models.[31] So, two strategies are necessary: listening to their voices and encouraging their curiosity continually. Students need teachers to listen to their questions and inquiries. It's important to validate their feelings rather than directly instructing. Help identify the thinking behind their doubtful and skeptical thoughts. Second, bolstering students' curiosity by building an inquisitive mind is another important strategy. In order to do that, provide a safe space for them to discuss texts, issues, truth, and problems throughout class. Teachers may develop critical thinking skills using varied pedagogy, engaging students' hearts as well as their heads. To be more effective, evaluations must consider the students' affective domain, which includes values, attitudes, and preferences. In order to do that, Otieno[32] recommends teachers take the role of a success coach. Success coaches provide a single primary person charged with more responsibilities, protecting a student's physical, emotional, and psychological safety to promote their cultural safety and healing from trauma to build a culture of care.

Gaining Community Actualization

A student's individual healthy doubt and skepticism can be transferred to organizational skepticism in which all students can actively participate and

30. Whitin and Whitin, "Learning Is Born of Doubting," 129.
31. Otieno, "Learning and Inquiry."
32. Otieno, "Learning and Inquiry."

develop a certain inquiry process. Each student's skepticism calls for mutuality and accountability in their community. So, teachers may have students collaborate in the learning experience in a team. This allows students to take ownership of their learning, while thinking critically about issues. Students are able to think about their own bias and perspective and that of their peers. When students collaborate together, they learn how to communicate with others effectively, work as a team, practice self-discipline, and improve social and interpersonal skills. Through collaboration, students are able to have a better understanding of what they are learning and improve critical thinking skills.

To bolster students' healthy doubt and skepticism, teachers may lead inquiry in two stages. First, have each student debate his or her position on a given issue or problem (individual inquiry level), then go to the collaborative inquiry in which students build upon one another's ideas in an attempt to clarify understandings and arrive at a shared and new or expanded way of thinking. Doubt-driven questions ignite student interest and can be springboards to class discussions that enable students to think critically about their personal stance on an issue while engaging in deep learning. These types of discussions, when pursued skillfully and respectfully, serve as practice fields for citizens and are needed to preserve, protect, and advance our democratic institutions.

The teacher's role as a bias sensor for this process is crucial. The role as a bias sensor is to determine whether or not sources, materials, and information is real, authentic, and impartial. In many classrooms, students are not comfortable expressing doubts and raising questions that catalyze and sustain discussion.

CONCLUDING REMARKS: "UNLESS I . . . "

Doubt and skepticism have not been embraced in the classroom positively, however, they are key critical skills needed in the twenty-first century based on a deep understanding of the nature and value of truth. By playing around with alternatives on their own terms, students gain a clear understanding and find the truth. Students are now searching for the truth by touching, grasping, and seeing it vividly and authentically, not handed down by authority. Through the healthy doubting and skeptical process, students may surpass their level of intellectual development, which moves through four stages: dualism, multiplicity, relativism, and commitment.[33] Paul describes this change process using the analogy from seeing in the mirror to seeing face to face in 1 Corinthians 13:10–12, which reads: "When completeness comes, what is in part disappears. When I was a child, I talked like a child, I thought like a child, I reasoned like a child. When I became a man, I put the ways of childhood behind me. For now, we see only a reflection as in a mirror; then we shall see face to face. Now I know in part; then I shall know fully, even as I am fully known."

33. Perry, "Achievement Gap."

9

Thriveology for the Competitive

Blessed are the peacemakers, for they will be called children of God.

(MATTHEW 5:9)

INTRODUCTION

THE CURRENT EDUCATION CLIMATE is designed to meet the needs of our capitalistic society. School curriculum is narrowly organized based on different contents and students are sorted by fiercely competitive, norm-based assessments through which only winners are rewarded. Students are to be seated quietly, obeying the teacher's directions. Classroom rules must be strictly observed. If a student breaks the rule, the student must be punished. In this environment, students are competitive, self-centered, and competitive against their colleagues to receive better grades. Our education has been too focused on meeting individual needs. Now it is time to switch our educational focus to building a community through collaborative, humbly serving spirits. How do we switch the learning environment from a competitive climate to a collaborative and community-actualizing climate? Based on the story of Jesus' teaching his disciples who argue, I will address effective strategies geared toward community-actualizing learning processes.

DISCIPLES' OF JESUS WHO ARE PRIDEFUL AND RIVALRY

Even after more than two years with their master, the twelve disciples of Jesus still remained competitive amongst themselves. In Luke 9:46, an argument started among them as to which of them would be the greatest. There are many times in the Bible where the disciples argue with each other regarding the same issue: who is the greatest among themselves (Luke 9:46; Matthew 20:24; Luke 22:24). This argument continued throughout Jesus' three years of ministry. Now, the time came for Jesus to teach his disciples the true meaning of greatness, where Jesus patiently reasoned with them about servant leadership.

Jesus knew their thoughts (Luke 9:47). He knew their hearts, which were full of pride and rivalry among themselves. The disciples were privileged to be with the master who performed miracles, wonders, and amazing things. Each disciple tried to set himself up at the top of the kingdom Jesus would establish. Or, they were very interested in the leadership position after Jesus. They saw other disciples as rivals to that role. Rather than building up their spiritual capacities, they were interested in the other disciples' standings. Peter, James, and John must have believed that they were preferred above the other disciples since they were part of Jesus' inner circle. Yet, among the three men, they were curious about the others' destiny. Peter asked Jesus, "What about him [John]?" (John 21:21). All ten disciples were indignant when Salome came to Jesus and asked him for a high position for her two sons (Matthew 20:21). The disciples of Jesus were jealous, envious, and selfish.

Who is great? Perhaps this is a critical issue even in contemporary education. We educate all students to be great. Yet, we don't have a consensus about the term. How do we define the term "great"? What are the criteria to measure greatness in students: by GPA, based on test scores? Are we sure that intelligence is greater than other measures?

Jesus identified the term "greatness" with a different perspective. Being great is the reverse of the greater humbly serving the lesser. He took a little child to stand in a place of honor next to him, saying, "Do you have enough humility to take a child seriously for my sake?" We see the same in John 13:4–5, where he demonstrated greatness by washing his disciples' feet. He taught by demonstrating an act of true humility to his arguing disciples. This is a paradox. Humility and servanthood are signs of greatness. Jesus taught that humility is honored rather than self-aggrandizing pride.

TWO EDUCATION PARADIGMS

Pride and rivalry, in fact, characterize the education paradigm in our capitalistic society, where education is designed to meet the needs of mass-production manufacturing systems. Schools are institutions that prepare young people for their place in the currently existing competitive market economy after equipping them with certain levels of cognitive capabilities.[1] Students in this paradigm are treated like empty vessels that are to be filled with knowledge and skills. Education is offered at the same pace using the same materials by meeting at the same classroom regularly. Uniformity, control, and centralization are core virtues by which all students are closely supervised based on rigid rules and discipline. Ignoring the value of diversity and individual differences, classroom cultures emphasize a standardized way of thinking.[2]

In this educational paradigm (see the modernism education paradigm in the table on the next page), schools function as a factory for reproducing the existing dominant social structures and ideological conditions. Apple[3] emphasizes the importance of the explicit curriculum in the reproduction of consciousness in capitalistic societies. The hidden curriculum also reproduces the attitudes and personality traits upon which work in capitalist society depends.[4] Bourdieu[5] asserts that in a classroom, the cultural capital of students who occupy a marginalized ethnicity are systematically devalued. Evaluation in this paradigm is mainly to sort high-performing students from low-performing students, in which efficiency has dictated a central core model leading to a too thinly defined outcome for student success. There is a clear demarcation line between winners and losers, and the winners take it all. Palmer clearly identifies the characteristics of today's education:

> Today education has become a training ground for competition. In fact, education itself has become a competitive arena where winners and losers are determined even before the contest of adult life begins. It is not only that when students get together to collaborate on their homework, many schools call it 'cheating' so suspect are

1. Giroux, *Teachers as Intellectuals.*
2. Reich, "Education and the Next Economy."
3. Apple, *Education and Power.*
4. Bowles and Gintis, *Schooling in Capitalist America*; McLaren, *Life in Schools.*
5. Bourdieu, "Systems of Education."

the communal virtues. It is not only that adults often insist that children who are educated to cooperate rather than compete are not well prepared for the real world. Beneath these symptoms lies the fact that the function of modern schools is more economic than cultural. They provide one more reminder that we should count not on communal support but on our individual survival skills.[6]

Competitive and self-oriented school climates may not meet the current postmodern needs in which diverse racial, cultural, and language-background students work cooperatively and productively in school.[7] Especially in the postmodern age, the paradigm of education has to change from standardization to customization,[8] from a focus on presenting standardized material to a focus on meeting the individual students' needs and backgrounds. Recognizing students' diverse cultural backgrounds and encouraging individual students' differences and values is important for ensuring meaningful learning experiences for all students. The table below is the summary of the difference between the modern and postmodern education paradigms.

Table 9.1: Differences between the Modern and Postmodern Education Paradigms

Criteria	Modern education paradigm	Postmodern education paradigm
Values pursued	Standardization, compliance, conformity, bureaucracy, efficiency, logical thinking	Customization, creativity, diversity, autonomy, excitement, effectiveness, critical thinking
Education service to super-system	To produce workers in order to meet the needs of capitalistic society	To facilitate student's meaningful learning to maximize individual capacity in community

6. Palmer, *Promise of Paradox*, 70.

7. J. Banks and C. Banks, *Multicultural Education*.

8. Marx, *Sixteen Trends*.

Role of education	Dissemination of information; remembering facts, information	Active process of discovering truth; expanding personal worldview via critical thinking
What is learning	Conveying particular piece of information, knowledge; learning is a transferred activity from teacher to students	Discovering underlined principles; learning is something constructed based on student's context and situation
The relationship between teacher and students	The teacher is a knowledge provider and source of information; the students are knowledge receivers	The teacher is a guide to information; teacher and students produce knowledge collaboratively and share creatively

Sadly, schooling has little changed since its inception, and it has become increasingly evident that the educational needs within our current society are not adequately satisfied by schools as they are now organized.[9] How can we lead the change in education and schooling to meet new social and cultural needs? Think about what Jesus said in Matthew 18:3: "Unless you change and become like little children . . . " He asked us to change our perspective from the traditional viewpoint to a new value system. Taking a child and putting them in a place of honor is the paradox by which he asked his disciples to humbly embrace a low status in the world for the sake of kingdom.

How do we switch from a competitive, isolated spirit in the classroom to a committed, collaborative learning environment where all students are eagerly working together as a community? How can a teacher assist students to be a part of a collaborative community? I will explain key strategies toward this aim using the CARING process.

9. Halbhavi et al., "Leadership Imperative."

CARING TOWARD COMMUNITY ACTUALIZING PROCESS

Too much of education has focused on meeting individual needs; I called this paradigm a self-fulfilling education. Education and schooling mainly functions for students (learners) to promote their social and economic status or to inform their personal well-being. In this approach, the classroom as a place of competition among colleagues and educational success means trampling on other students based on norm-referencing evaluation, demonstrating better knowledge, competencies, and skills than other students in the classroom. Even emphasizing collaboration among students becomes an empty educational goal in this setting because a true community can be built only through three key characteristics: 1) mutual engagement, 2) joint enterprise, and 3) a shared repertoire of communal resources.[10] A mutual engagement of participants allows them to do what they need to do and binds members into a social entity. A joint enterprise results from a collective process of negotiation that reflects the full complexity of mutual engagement. A shared repertoire of communal resources belongs to the community of practice that the community produced or adopted in the course of its existence. Michael Hester[11] lists several qualities of community: growth in intimacy; covenant love that is intentional, incarnational, conflictual, encouraging, and intimate; and the ability for sensitive and creative listening. How would teachers build true community in the classroom?

Cultivating Connections

"Knowing their thoughts . . . " (Luke 9:47). This was the starting point of Jesus' teaching. He knew his disciples' prideful rivalry and competitive attitude toward each other, which hinders building a community of wholeness. A master teacher has keen eyes to identify the cause of their students' behaviors which are hidden. Jesus did not publicly criticize them or lecture them to be humble in their behaviors and speech. Instead, he took a little child to stand beside him, gently saying that the least is the greatest.

Using a child to teach the real meaning of greatness is symbolic. A vast array of differences existed between a child and his disciples. A child represents a genuine, undisputable, authentic attitude, while the disciples are

10. Wenger, *Community of Practice*.

11. Hester, "Theology for Family Ministry," 165.

competitive and prideful. A child was considered as lowly and weak with little importance or esteem in Hebrew culture, while the disciples wanted to be great leaders with power and prestige. The disciples wanted to build the community based on an organizational, hierarchical position of title, power, and status, while children dream of a community full of humble service, welcome, loving people, and caring individuals.

There are many ways to cultivate impactful connections that teachers can utilize. They can take any object, any place, any issue or context to motivate students to learn actively. Teaching is a creative and insightful intervention through which students open their minds to learn in order to change their lives.

Affirming Personhood: Strength-Based Approach

Each person has his/her own quality and uniqueness. Jesus identified the innate unique quality in children. Traditional education sees children as blank sheets to be filled with new information, skills, and knowledge. In this paradigm, education takes a deficit-based model, identifying first students' needs, problems, cognitive gaps, and discrepancies before class begins. However, educators learn that recognizing students' assets, strengths, and interests is essential to lead to effective learning. This is called a strengths-based approach, which is particularly important when working with diverse and vulnerable student populations, including ethnically, linguistically, and culturally diverse students.[12] It is beneficial for students to promote a sense of belonging because this approach emphasizes the positive aspects of student effort, achievement, and strengths.[13] Especially regarding students with traumatic and vulnerable experiences, a strengths-based approach believes that the human brain has a great capacity to build new pathways for being and acting.[14]

In order to implement strengths-based models effectively, the first task that teachers need to implement is a universal screening process through which they can identify each student's strengths and assets from the beginning of the school year. Based on the students' data, teachers can

12. Seligman et al., "Positive Psychotherapy"; Biswas-Dienera et al., "Dynamic Approach."

13. Lopez and Louis, "Principles of Strengths-Based Education"; Clifton et al., *StrengthsQuest.*

14. Zacarian et al., *Teaching to Strengths.*

personalize the learning experience by practicing individualization, whereby they think about and act upon the strengths of each student, fostering development and integration of new behaviors associated with positive outcomes.[15]

Restoring Relationships

How can we create a classroom culture in which all students are connected and committed to maximize their potential in their learning experiences? How can we free ourselves from the old paradigm where students are isolated and highly competitive in adversarial relationships with each other? Swell[16] suggests a new learning environment in which students comprehensively connect in four relationships: physical, intellectual, emotional, and social connections.

Intellectual connections are apparent when students and teachers respond to each other's ideas using a dialogue of knowledge building through which they discover new understandings collaboratively. Social connections function productively when students and teachers are co-decision-makers for learning and classroom activities to balance power in relationships, and when they bring their out-of-school experiences to the classroom. Emotional connections are observed in their mutual respect, trust, and honesty and in their authentic expression of feelings, emotions, and concerns as caring relations. Physical connections are seen when teachers and children begin to share the classroom space in more non-hierarchical, horizontal classroom structures and organizations. The key factor for bonding the four connections strongly together is the students' deep sense of identity and authenticity from which students connect with others unselfconsciously and selflessly.[17]

---

15. Lopez and Louis, "Principles of Strengths-Based Education."
16. Sewell, "Evoking Children's Spirituality."
17. Sewell, "Evoking Children's Spirituality."

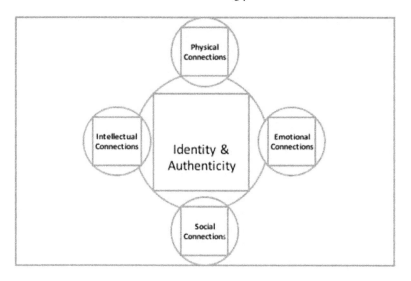

Figure 9.1: Four Connections to Build a Positive Classroom Environment[/CAP}

Initiating Inquiry: Learning through Paradox

It is a paradox. Jesus took a little child to teach his prideful disciples the true meaning of greatness. Learning through paradox is a powerful method. It is a pedagogical strategy for exploring contradictions and complexity in order to change students' inner perspective or to gain new learning. In fact, Jesus used paradoxes frequently when he delivered his messages. For example: "For whoever wants to save their life will lose it, but whoever loses their life . . . will save it" (Mark 8:35); "whoever wants to become great . . . must be your servant, and whoever wants to be first must be slave of all" (Mark 10:43–44).

What is a paradox? It is contradictory, mutually exclusive elements that exist simultaneously and for which no synthesis or choice is possible or necessarily desirable.[18] Paradox exists as mixed messages, conflicting demands, or opposing perspectives,[19] or a creative tension like the two ends of the magnet that never touch.[20] In fact, teachers encounter many

18. Cameron and Quinn, "Organizational Paradox and Transformation," 2.

19. Lewis and Dehler, "Learning through Paradox," 710.

20. Palmer, *Courage to Teach*, 77.

common paradoxes in their teaching. They confront at least six paradoxes and contradiction in their everyday teaching contexts:[21]

- Control and flow: teachers are in control of course content but also go with the flow.
- Facilitator and evaluator: teachers develop trusting relationships with students but also judge students' progress.
- Loving the subject and loving the students: teachers are devoted to their own learning of the subject but also committed to their students' learning of the subject.
- Subject expert and teaching/learning expert: teachers know their disciplines but also know the learning process for a diverse array of students.
- Caring for students and caring for self: teachers love both self and others (students) at the same time.
- Individual mentor and group learning leader: teachers serve both the group as a whole and the individual learners in the group.

Palmer[22] also identifies six paradoxes that teachers experience while teaching in a classroom space:

- The space should be bounded and open.
- The space should be hospitable and charged.
- The space should invite the voice of the individual and the voice of the group.
- The space should honor the little stories of the students and the big stories of the disciplines and tradition.
- The space should support solitude and surrounded it with the resources of the community.
- The space should welcome both silence and speech.

Using paradoxes in teaching is beneficial in many ways. First, paradoxes help students understand the complex nature of a certain issue, human life, and educational phenomena. It allows students to comprehend the learning process as new frames fuel their own contradictions and tensions,

21. Robertson, "Integrity in Learner-Centered Teaching."
22. Palmer, *Courage to Teach*, 76.

stimulating further and deeper discoveries.[23] Secondly, teaching through paradoxes heralds a shift from the teaching paradigm (teacher centered) to the learning paradigm (learner centered). Paradox gives students ill-defined issues and problems where students develop, create, and discover new insights, perceptions, and solutions through collaborative dialogue and praxis process among themselves.[24]

How can we use paradox in education? Knight and Paroutis[25] suggest a set of four stages of teaching with paradox using the concept "threshold" as a basis from which teachers can develop appropriate interventions to assist with student learning of paradox. The four stages are: 1) setting up the right context of learning in which teachers carefully select cohort based on diverse backgrounds; 2) shaping the content that students are exposed to in which students identify appropriate problems that are crucial to paradoxi-cal tensions; 3) setting up an experiential process by pursuing new ideas and a creative perspective to respond to paradoxical tensions; and 4) creating space for critical reflection, examining specific issues arising in relation to paradoxical tensions. The figure below is a brief depiction of the process.

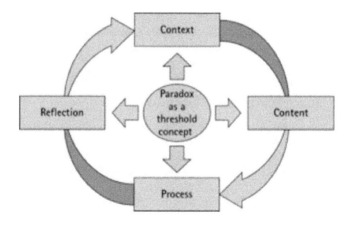

Figure 9.2: A Model for Using Paradox as a Threshold Concept in Education[26]

---

23. Robertson, "Generative Paradox"; Lewis and Dehler, *Learning through Paradox*.

24. Knight and Paroutis, *Expanding the Paradox-Pedagogy Links*; Lewis and Dehler, "Learning through Paradox."

25. Knight and Paroutis, "Expanding the Paradox-Pedagogy Links," 537.

26. Knight and Paroutis, "Expanding the Paradox-Pedagogy Links," 537.

So, how do we develop the paradox in our teaching setting? Robertson[27] suggests developing an attitude to embrace paradox more positively, such as:

- We need to appreciate or value paradox.

- We need to resist the impulse to try to resolve paradoxes; they just are, and we should get over it.

- We need to look beyond the dualistic logical premise.

- We need to listen and give credence to things that we know but cannot say; paradoxes are usually known best intuitively.

- We need to tolerate, even enjoy, ambiguity which often accompanies paradoxes; they are not neat and precise.

Nurturing SEL

A paradox-embedded pedagogy is learner centered in which students' reflective thinking is highly encouraged.[28] Paradoxes make students see their limitations and weaknesses more clearly and inspire them to make a community together to search for truth collaboratively. Exposing paradoxical tensions asks them to acknowledge the limitations of each person's perspective and embrace other's unique and creative viewpoints to embrace a collaborative community spirit. This community is called a "community of truth,"[29] which enables students to shift from an either-or toward a both-and perspective. In fact, there are many paradoxical situations teachers can bring into the classroom, such as equity versus equality, effectiveness versus efficiency, inclusion versus exclusion, multiculturalism versus nationalism, globalism versus localism, standards versus teacher autonomy, and yin and yang. By involving students in this kind of paradoxical situation, students eventually learn to integrate two opposing values by creating new concepts of learning enthusiastically and collaboratively. Not only do they gain new learning, but they also learn to respect the benefit of the opposing values, which makes their world larger, more generous, and more hopeful.[30]

27. Robertson, "Generative Paradox," 186–87.
28. Lewis and Dehler, "Learning through Paradox."
29. Palmer, *Courage to teach.*
30. Palmer, *Promise of Paradox.*

The purpose of learning through paradox is to change a student's perspective. Read what Jesus said in Mark 18:3: "Unless you change and become like children." Jesus asked his disciples to change and transform their mindsets. Unless they changed their cultural assumptions (their cultural view of the low status of children) and embraced the new value system toward children, they would not enter the kingdom. A new concept of greatness means a willingness to embrace a low status in the world and to humble oneself (to choose a lowly status).

While facilitating a lesson with paradoxes, teachers serve as a guide, not as a director, so that students fully express and share their thoughts, perspectives, reflections, and experiences with others. The role of the teacher as a guide is critical in order to create a culture of care in the classroom through which students feel a sense of connectedness, care, and nurture in relationships between the teacher and students and among students.[31] Caring involves a transposition of attentiveness from my reality to the reality of the other. Students try to put themselves in the shoes of the cared for to embrace their situation as closely as they can, as if it were their own.[32] Therefore, during paradox-embedded learning, teachers may allow a certain level of autonomy and freedom rather than practicing rigid standards in which students may decide progress by themselves.

Gaining Community Actualization

Traditional education has focused on improving cognitive capacities for each individual student. The result of education has been measured by each student's improved knowledge and skills. The education process has mainly focused on memorization by which all learning has been highly controlled in a competitive learning environment. In this paradigm, the classroom environment has been highly organized for efficiency, where authentic teamwork and collaboration may not be possible.

There are two opposing approaches to view the result of education: a self-fulfilling education and a community actualizing education. The former style is the industrial (modern)-age model and the latter is the information (postmodern)-age paradigm. The former was founded based on a scarcity mindset, while the latter was based on an abundance mindset. The former is deficit based; the latter represents a strength-oriented perspective. The

31. Vigil et al., "Developing Peacemakers."

32. Nodding, *Caring*.

purpose of the former model is to fill the academic gaps through teacher-led educational methods. Teachers consider students as a deficient person who needs to be mediated. The teacher in the latter paradigm, however, sees students as active agents to discover and create knowledge and skills both intrinsically and collaboratively. Students contribute to society utilizing their strengths and skills through acquiring the knowledge, skills, and attitudes allowing them to participate successfully in society. How do we change the educational paradigm from self-fulfilling to community actualizing? The table below is a summary of these two educational paradigms.

Table 9.3: Two Educational Paradigms

Descriptors	Self-fulfilling education	Community-actualizing education
Goals	Self-actualization, personal well-being, healing individual ailments, educating for individual socialization and enculturation	Community actualization, community well-being, educating for shalom and social justice
Target focused	Strengthens cognitive and academic skills, focus on intellectual issues	Strengthens non-cognitive skills, social emotional capacities, and spiritual capacity
Instructional methods	Lecture, individualized learning, differentiated instruction	Problem-solving through collaborative learning, praxis, culturally relevant, contextualization
Evaluation strategies	Reaction and learning evaluation	Application and impact on community, problem-solving
Relationships between teacher and students	Autocratic teacher, adversarial relationship between teacher and students	Incarnational and reformational teacher, co-agents discover together during the learning process

Education is an intentional activity through which students gain knowledge of themselves in relationship to others and the community in which they live.[33] In community-actualizing education, all people and cultures are linked together in unity, contributing to the whole society with their unique qualities and gifts. Therefore, education is an intentional intervention through which everyone shows love and compassion to each other as well as promotes equality and justice among all people. This kind of relationship is described beautifully in Isaiah 11:6–9:

> The wolf will live with the lamb, the leopard will lie down with the goat, the calf and the lion and the yearling together; and a little child will lead them. The cow will feed with the bear, their young will lie down together, and the lion will eat straw like the ox. The infant will play near the cobra's den, and the young child will put its hand into the viper's nest. They will neither harm nor destroy on all my holy mountain, for the earth will be filled with the knowledge of the LORD as the waters cover the sea.

CONCLUSION: EDUCATION IS A PEACEMAKING PROCESS

Our schools rank and sort students and only the fittest students can succeed. Learning activities are creating a competitive, zero-sum game and the reinforcement of scarcity thinking injures real learning.[34] This school system views all students the same, asking students to obey rigid rules and policies with behaviorism-based disciplines, such as reinforcement and punishment. Students' behaviors are managed and shaped based on predefined educational goals and classroom procedures. Only students who pass can survive and this kind of classroom environment, which makes all students rivals and competitors.

The classroom is a place where many unexpected conflicts occur, both academic as well as social. Peace is not the absence of conflict, but it is the ability to handle it by peaceful means. Yes, we don't need to destroy all conflicts in the classroom by controlling students with strict rules; we need to educate students about how to solve conflicts more creatively and collaboratively. Now is the time to equip all students to be peacemakers, taking care

33. Knight, *Philosophy and Education*.
34. Palmer, *Courage to Teach*.

of others and our communities in a collaborative learning environment. Peacemaking is an ongoing process through which students build trust, heal harm to relationships, restore the dignity of persons affected, respect multiculturalism, be aware of differences, and create safety.[35] Throughout this peacemaking process, students may change their perspective of greatness from position, power, and title to humbling themselves, serving the weak, and taking care of the community's needs. That's why Jesus asked us to be peacemakers. "Blessed are the peacemakers, for they will be called children of God" (Matthew 5:9).

---

35. Vigil et al., "Developing Peacemakers," 82.

10

Thriveology for the Discriminated Student

Blessed are those who are persecuted because of righteousness, for theirs is the kingdom of heaven.

(MATTHEW 5:10)

INTRODUCTION

EDUCATIONAL INEQUITIES HAVE CONTRIBUTED to a crisis of collective and individual trauma for students, particularly for Black and Latinx students.[1] Even though this country has exerted ongoing efforts to fulfill educational equality and equity for all students, the achievement gap remains unchanged.[2] Disparity exists between test scores of white students and minorities, primarily African American and Hispanic students, who are at risk of false positives, or being falsely identified as having a disability.[3] Many EL students in special education classes only lack in English proficiency and have been misdiagnosed due to improper testing or assessment bias.[4] These students are now labeled as inferior, which carries not only educational ramifications but social ones well. It is far easier for teachers

1. Grant and Sleeter, "Race, Class, Gender."
2. DomNwachukwu, *Introduction to Multicultural Education*.
3. Harry, "Minority Disproportionality."
4. Pazos-Rego, "Learning Disabilities."

and administrators to blame the students themselves rather than examine the testing process or its damaging effects.[5] How can we implement an equity pedagogy through which we build a more democratic and equal educational environment by closing the achievement as well as discipline gaps in school? In this chapter, after reviewing Jesus' teaching to marginalized people, I will share the urgency of implementing equity pedagogy in classrooms.

TEACHING A MARGINALIZED PERSON

There is an unnamed Samaritan woman in John 4 who had been discriminated against by her community. In fact, she was triple victimized: 1) she married five times, and currently lived with another man, which was considered to be living in sin, which was condemned by her community; 2) she was a Samaritan, a member of the hated mixed race who had been disregarded, a race traditionally despised by Jews; and 3) she was a woman, representing the lowest of the low, a female in a society where women were demeaned. These circumstances point to her desire to avoid the shame that would come by attending the well when other women were present. Most women drew water in groups in the morning, and it was often a social occasion. However, she was drawing water alone at noon, which indicates that she was a social outcast.

When Jesus was left alone at the well while disciples were out to buy something to eat, he encountered this woman. Jesus taught amazingly, and she was changed and healed. How did Jesus teach this woman? What methods did Jesus use to transform her perspective? Jesus used the discovery model in this particular encounter. Lee[6] identifies four stages of the discovery teaching method: 1) identifying teachable moments, 2) guiding inquiry with intriguing questions, 3) allowing exploration of a hypothesis, and 4) encouraging application.

5. Nieto and Body, *School Reform*.
6. Lee, "Jesus' Teaching through Discovery."

Figure 10.1: Discovery Teaching Process

First, Jesus was a master teacher who identified the exact time to teach a particular student a specific topic. In this case, he knew the needs and assets of the Samaritan woman. A Jewish man wouldn't talk to a woman; however, Jesus provided a space for her in which she shared her agony and pain. Teaching is our intentional effort to break the wall that separates students based on race, gender, ethnicity, religion, and disability etc., and to build bridges where all students may meet each other. Jesus knew the Samaritan woman's needs and desires for water on a deeper level, such as her desire for a satisfying marriage, a spiritual yearning to be saved, and a healing from her ruined life. Again, this was the right time to accept the message of Jesus through which she would be transformed.

Second, he opened the inquiry with the question, "Could you give me a drink?" He acknowledged the woman by providing an opportunity for service. Jesus was thirsty, and she had water to give. From that moment, the relationship between a stranger (Jesus) and a Samaritan woman changed to that of a teacher (Jesus) and a student (the woman). He took the opportunity to explain his mission by using the context of the situation (living water). Jesus made a creative transition from known (the physical water, the immediate) to unknown (the spiritual, living water, the eternal), from physical quench to spiritual satisfaction. This is the second stage of a discovery learning process.

Third, Jesus allowed the Samaritan woman to explore a hypothesis through a discovery. Jesus began dialogue with her by raising a physical need, but quickly directed the conversation toward her spiritual need that could be quenched. "Sir, give me this water so that I won't get thirsty" (John 4:15). This was a turning point for her to discover the truth. Good teaching is not taking away challenges, but empowering students to deal with their challenges from what they learn. This is a constructive struggling process, but it is necessary to gain new insights. She now searched her life and acknowledged who Jesus is: "I can see that you are a prophet" (John 4:19). The Samaritan woman knew the truth and experienced total freedom and healing. She found the truth and met the Messiah (John 4:26).

Finally, she left her water pot at the well and ran back to the city to exclaim her joy (yes, the result of a teaching should be joy). Learning is powerful! When true and authentic learning occurs, all students are freed and delighted. The message of hope, restoration, healing, and new insights fill students' hearts. Students now confront fear, oppression, and injustice, and they are willing to break all walls of hostility, separation, and isolation. The woman was now freed and proclaimed what she had found and learned. The powerful effect of learning is to transform students' lives by applying what they learn. Education is more than teaching facts and learning the reasons so we can manipulate life toward our ends.[7] It means being drawn into personal responsiveness and accountability to each other and the world of which we are a part.

EQUITY PEDAGOGY IN CLASSROOM

Traditionally, American education has focused on educational equality, which emphasizes treating all students the same, expecting the same outcomes and achievement for all students. Equality in education means offering every student the same curriculum, instruction, and evaluation. However, this focus has resulted in many negative effects on students' learning. The curriculum in most schools is dominated by a Eurocentric or white frame of reference, which conveys that Eurocentric experiences are the most valued and central in education.[8] The current pattern of minority overrepresentation in special education programs is problematic, in

7. Palmer, *To Know as We Are Known*, 14.

8. Hyland, "Social Justice."

which marginalized populations may be receiving inequitable treatment.[9] African American and Hispanic students are at risk of false positives or being falsely identified as having a disability.[10] These students are labeled as inferior so that teachers and administrators easily blame the students themselves rather than examine the testing process or its damaging effects.[11]

Now teachers understand that treating all students the same does not guarantee academic success for all students. They are sensitive to focusing on ensuring that each student has the opportunity to develop their skills based on their cultural values. Equity pedagogy is essential for teachers to turn into an action through which teachers provide equal and fair education among/between students.[12] Banks defines equity pedagogy as "teaching strategies and classroom environments that help students from diverse racial, ethnic, and cultural groups to attain the knowledge, skills and attitudes needed to function effectively within and to help create and perpetuate a just, humane and democratic society."[13]

Hence, equity pedagogy places teachers in a challenging situation as they are required to use teaching strategies that suit the learning of different students so that all students may have the ability to enthusiastically achieve their learning goals. Therefore, the goal of equity pedagogy is to build each student's self-efficacy.[14] Teachers may develop their instructional strategies to achieve educational goals for students who have diverse and marginalized backgrounds.[15] How would teachers implement equity pedagogy through which all students, regardless of their differences and diversities in terms of language, gender, ethnicities, SES etc., achieve learning goals? Here, I will address four approaches of equity pedagogy, which are: culturally relevant teaching, critical pedagogy, social justice education, and complex instruction.

9. Vigil et al., "Developing Peacemakers."

10. Harry, "Minority Disproportionality."

11. Nieto and Body, *School Reform*.

12. Hammond, *Culturally Responsive Teaching*; Unterhalter, "What Is Equity in Education?"

13. J. Banks, *Educating Citizens*, 92–93.

14. J. Banks, "Multicultural Education," 18.

15. C. Banks and J. Banks, "Equity Pedagogy."

Culturally Relevant Teaching

Using children's personal and cultural knowledge as the basis of teaching promotes educational equity.[16] In order to implement culturally relevant teaching, teachers may consider four factors in their teaching: awareness, information processing, learning partnership, and community building.[17]

Critical Pedagogy

Critical pedagogy investigates injustice in multiple categories (race, class, gender, religion, etc.) in everyday school and classroom practices. Critical theorists often focus on the marginalized in the schools and expose how systems of power attempt to control schools through curriculum. By recognizing the hidden curriculum, critical theorists hope to alert teachers and students of the ways they are being manipulated by those who hope to maintain power in schools.[18] Henry Giroux posits, "critical pedagogy is informed by a political project that links education to the struggle for a public life in which dialogue, vision, and compassion are attentive to the rights and conditions that organize public life as a democratic social form rather than as a regime for terror and oppression."[19]

It is essential that teachers help students see that gender, class, race, culture, and ethnicity can be expressed in diverse ways, and teachers can engage all children in the class in exploring issues of fairness and justice and thinking about their role in making a more just world for themselves and others.[20] The three main instructional methods of critical pedagogy include: 1) dialogue, which is essential for democratic relationships; 2) praxis, which is necessary for social change; and 3) contextualization, which addresses the student's reality.[21] The call for a dialogical approach concurs with postmodern recognition of knowledge as a social construct in which teachers and students collaborate in the knowledge-making process.[22] Critical pedagogy has the task of educating students to become crit-

---

16. Hammond, *Culturally Responsive Teaching*; Hyland, "Social Justice."
17. Hammond, *Culturally Responsive Teaching*.
18. Lee and Givens, "Critical Consciousness."
19. Giroux, "Democracy, Education, and Politics," 82.
20. Giroux, "Democracy, Education, and Politics."
21. Lee and Givens, "Critical Consciousness."
22. DomNachukwu and Lee, *Multiculturalism*.

ical agents who actively question and negotiate the relationships between theory and practice, critical analysis and common sense, and learning and social change.[23] Fobes and Kaufman[24] identify several characteristics of critical pedagogy:

- Encourages the eradication of the teacher-student contradiction whereby the teacher teaches and the students are taught; the teacher is the subject and the students are mere objects;

- Promotes a problem-solving dialogue (instead of a banking/lecturing style) that emanates from the lived experiences (generative themes) of the learners;

- Fosters epistemological curiosity in both teachers and learners;

- Strives for praxis: reflection and action of the social world in order to transform it.

Social Justice Education

Young[25] deconstructs the large category of oppression into a set of conditions that are shared by people who suffer inhibition of their ability to develop and exercise their capacities and express their needs, thoughts, and feelings. She identifies the five faces of oppression: 1) exploitation, 2) marginalization, 3) powerlessness, 4) cultural imperialism, and 5) violence. Oppression represents a variety of forms in current societal constructs, such as racism, tracking, stereotype, microaggression, social injustice, etc. There are many examples of microaggressions committed by unaware individuals in the implementation of school procedures for student placement into special education, tracking, and unequal application of discipline.[26]

Social justice education examines the impact that power, privilege, and social oppression have on social groups and promotes social and political action as a means to gain equity for all citizens.[27] The desired outcome of social justice education is for students to be responsible social actors in order to transform social issues, such as educational inequity, racism,

23. Giroux, "Democracy, Education, and Politics."
24. Forbes and Kaufman, "Critical Pedagogy," 26–27.
25. Young, *Social Justice and Politics*, 40.
26. Saphier, "Equitable Classroom," 30.
27. Picower, "Using Their Words."

dehumanization, and oppression.[28] Four characteristics of social justice education are being collaborative, democratic, participatory, and inclusive.[29]

First, social justice education is collaborative. It pursues an integrated solution that relies on many forms of student-family-school-community collaboration.[30] The action plan will be examined at the individual, cultural, and institutional levels of society.[31] It emphasizes connecting communities together to have a sense of social responsibility toward and with others, their society, and the broader world in which we live. Therefore, social justice education is a community-centered, problem-based collaborative effort.[32] It is also democratic. Social justice educators use culturally relevant content to examine multiple forms of oppression to increase students' sociocultural awareness.[33] Students examine the work of the coalition through the lenses of rights-based, representational, and participatory discourses of democratic practice.[34] Furthermore, social justice education is participatory. It is an inquiry-based process that facilitates students' critical thinking skills with critical questions such as "Who benefits?"; "Who is marginalized?"; and "Why is a practice fair or unfair?"[35] Finally, social justice education is inclusive. Teachers build equitable classrooms where students care and respect each other's perspective.[36] While discussing issues, students' diverse perspectives and values are shared. They raise awareness and support for their issues, answering questions such as "How could it be different?" and "What kind of society would I like to live in and how could I get there?"[37]

Social justice education emphasizes explicit curricular content related to social identity and injustice, oppression theory, intersectionality, and reflexive teaching practice.[38] How can we implement social justice education in a class? Darling-Hammond[39] suggests that teachers for social justice

28. Woodrow, "Practicing Social Justice Education."
29. Adams, *Social Justice Education*, 1036.
30. Gardner and Cockwell, *Engaging Democracy*.
31. Hardiman et al., *Conceptual Foundation*.
32. Woodrow, *Practicing Social Justice Education*.
33. Adams, "Social Justice Education"; Picower, "Using Their Words."
34. Gardner and Crockwell, "Engaging Democracy."
35. Dover, "Teaching for Social Justice."
36. Picower, "Using Their Words."
37. Golden and Fink, "Conversation with Linda Christensen," 61.
38. Dover, "Teaching for Social Justice."
39. Darling-Hammond, "Educating the New Educator."

need to understand students' identity, their background, and worldviews as well as the sources of inequities and privileges, so that they create a project to raise awareness and support for their issues. Crosby, Howell, and Thomas[40] summarize the practical strategies for implementing social justice in classrooms: 1) teachers need to establish regular classroom routines that are consistently followed, where transitions or changes to the routine are discussed with students in advance in order to maintain dependability; 2) teachers need to exercise patience and empathy when students act out during a transitional time or unexpected routine change; 3) teachers need to take intentional steps to remove potential triggers from the classroom; 4) teachers need to have safety plans in place for identified students in order to be prepared when difficult student behavior surfaces; 5) teachers need to have regular class meetings to discuss safety, particularly after weekends and holidays; 6) teachers need to embed opportunities into the class routine for students to have some measure of control.

Complex Instruction

A student's status is deeply ingrained in academic achievement, which becomes the basis for their expectations for competence: low expectations for low-status students and high expectations for high-status students.[41] How can we minimize the problem of unequal access and learning for low-status students? Complex instruction is designed to broaden the conception of what it means to be smart, especially for low-status students. Using cooperative learning designed to promote equity, teachers may intervene to equalize rates of participation to close the academic achievement gap between those two groups of students.[42] Teachers can assign open-ended, interdependent group activities in which students not only decide what to include but also how to structure their product to best reflect the topic they are studying.[43] Students collaboratively explore alternative solutions to inherently uncertain tasks/issues, examining them from different perspectives, justifying their arguments, and developing higher-order thinking.

---

40. Crosby et al., "Social Justice Education," 21.
41. Cohen et al., "Complex Instruction"; Cohen et al., "Can Expectations."
42. Bannister, "Breaking the Spell."
43. Cohen et al., "Complex Instruction."

Complex instruction mainly employs two strategies: 1) the multiple-abilities treatment and 2) assigning competence to low-status students.[44] Multiple-ability treatment is intentionally recognizing each student's different skills and intellectual abilities necessary to complete the particular learning task based on the conviction that there are different ways to be smart. Teachers intentionally orient their students to the many different intellectual abilities, skills, and competencies required in the task, so as to disrupt narrow conceptions of the discipline and broaden what it means to be smart.

Assigning competence is a powerful treatment in which teachers focus special attention on low-status students. Teachers boost the participation of low-status students by encouraging interaction between high- and low-status students.[45] Teachers recognize each student's intellectual contribution to the group task. Everyone is viewed as capable and competent, challenging the racialized hierarchies of perceived academic competence found in classrooms and larger society.

Is complex instruction an effective intervention to promote equity in the classroom? Even though this approach takes a deliberate attempt to disrupt enactments of social inequalities within the classroom, this approach shows two main flaws in nature. First, this approach takes social inequality for granted. This approach assumes that high-status individuals are expected to be more competent in classroom tasks than low-status students, which influences expectations for performance. The main purpose of this approach is to build a mutual relationship among students from diverse backgrounds. Students are engaged in learning activities cooperatively and seek their academic and relational success as the teacher designs. Therefore, this approach is teacher centered. Teachers practice through the lens of a status characteristics (gender, race, social class, academic ability, physical attractiveness, prior academic performance, etc.).[46] This approach seems lacking to equip students to be responsible agents to facilitate social change.

There are four approaches to promote equity pedagogy. The table below is a summary of four equity pedagogy approaches along with purpose, instructional strategies, strengths and concerns, and key theorists.

Table 10.1: Four Approaches of Equity Pedagogy

44. Cohen et al., "Complex Instruction"; Banister, "Breaking the Spell."
45. Cohen et al., "Complex Instruction"; Banister, "Breaking the Spell."
46. Bannister, "Breaking the Spell."

	Culturally responsive teaching	Social justice education	Critical pedagogy	Complex instruction
Purpose	Independent learning for agency	Educational reform and transformation	Educating students to become critical agents	Cultivating equal-status interactions in cooperative group settings
Instructional strategies	Improving the learning capacity of minority students to maximize their capacities, focusing on affective and cognitive domains of teaching and learning	Exposing the social, political context that students experience; equipping students with conscious competencies to solve educational inequality	Emphasizing dialogue, establishing praxis, contextualizing education	Multiple ability strategy, assigning competence, open-ended and uncertain tasks, problem-solving
Strengths and concerns	Building cognitive and academic mindset by pushing back on dominant narratives about people of color, focusing on minority's perspective, tend to see the world as a dichotomy and focus on the power struggle relationship between the majority and minority	Creating a lens to recognize and interrupt inequitable patterns and practices in society; there is no agreed definition and approach of social justice education	See education as instrumental (to lead a social change); the transition process is emphasized; the oppressed only can become the change agents to lead the social transformation	Improving human relations and social harmony among different social status, instructional methods without raising the questions about inequality, takes social inequality for granted
Theorists	Banks, J., Ladson-Billings, Grant, C. A, Sleeter, C. E.	Darling-Hammond; Christense, L; Nieto, S., bell hooks	Freire, P., Giroux, H., McLaren, P., Greene, M., J. Kozol	Cohen, E., and Lotan, R.

CARING: IMPLEMENTING EQUITY PEDAGOGY
IN A CLASSROOM

Education and schooling exist for pursuing equal opportunity for all children through which they fully develop their potentials on a commitment to social justice and the cultivation of democratic citizenship.[47] However, education is one of the most powerful institutions implicated in the process of reproducing social inequalities.[48] Students fail to achieve academic goals mainly because their cultural differences are not dealt with appropriately in their educational setting. Socioeconomic status plays an important role in a students' education and the achievement gap. Students who grow up in higher-income families obtain high achievement due to better equipped school environments, which tend to have many opportunities for extra-curricular activities, along with educated parents.[49] The current pattern of minority overrepresentation in special education programs is problematic because it represents yet another instance where marginalized populations may be receiving inequitable treatment. How do teachers handle this issue and provide an equitable pedagogy in their classrooms? In this section, I will address teaching strategies using the CARING processes.

Cultivating Connections

Education is a series of opportunities through which teachers can offer an appropriate connection with students who need educational interventions. Teachers' encounters with students are intentional and purposeful, not accidental occasions. Think about Jesus teaching the Samaritan woman in John 4. He intentionally sought to meet the woman at that specific time and place. He knew the woman's inner thirst, so he asked her, "Will you give me a drink?," which began a powerful connection with her. Similarly, teachers must intentionally cross barriers of attitude, fear, and embarrassment in order to establish relationships with students, especially those who are marginalized and isolated. In addition, teachers should understand the concept of culture as a key term in discourse about the teaching/learning process. Through a cultural lens, teachers recognize how power, history, and ethics are inextricably intertwined in each student's (and their family's)

47. Hytten and Bettez, *Understanding Education*.
48. Hart, *Education, Inequality*; Collins, *Social Reproduction in Classrooms*.
49. Persell, *Social Class*.

life. They use responsive teaching methods that affirm and respect students' different backgrounds and ways of knowing, including students' lived experiences, sociocultural backgrounds, and prior knowledge and values that students bring into the classroom. Regardless of their background, teachers must hold high expectations for students and engage them in a process of knowledge construction that challenges deficit thinking about marginalized groups.[50]

Affirming Personhood

It is crucial to create a culture of equity in a classroom where all students respect and value each other's work, and where everyone is respected and valued. In this kind of learning context, students understand the importance of maintaining their own cultural identity and heritage without losing sight of their academic achievement.[51] Dilard[52] identifies eight tenets to build a lovely community in a school and classroom:

1. A strong awareness that one is a citizen of the world;

2. An understanding that freedom is an internal desire in the soul of every person and is important to preserving our humanity;

3. Has a basis in nonviolence and acceptance;

4. An understanding that whatever affects one directly affects all indirectly;

5. A recognition that we are each unique in order to realize our need of one another;

6. An understanding that citizens must be judged not by the color of their skin but the content of their character;

7. An awareness that while all people have been psychologically damaged by the construct of race, Blacks must no longer be ashamed of being black;

8. An emphasis on dignifying all labor, understanding the role of economics and social class.

50. Diaz-Rico and Weed, *Cross-Cultural Language*.
51. Ruiz and Cantu, *Teaching the Teachers*.
52. Dillard, *You Are Because I Am*, 135.

Restoring Relationships

Jesus knew the personal agony and painful history of the woman, which restores a positive relationship with her. In order to restore relationships, two competencies need to be equipped by equity pedagogy teachers. First, they must use culturally responsive teaching methods that affirm and respect students' different backgrounds and ways of knowing. Teachers are cultural workers. Students' lived experiences, cultural backgrounds, and prior knowledge are used to design instruction that illustrates the value of what students bring to the classroom.[53] Teachers hold high expectations for students and engage them in a process of knowledge construction that challenges deficit thinking about marginalized groups.[54]

Secondly, teachers need to fully understand the issues of systemic racism, social injustice and oppression, and microaggression based on race, social class, gender, and disability. They possess the ability to critically investigate the ways in which educational inequality should not be reproduced through school curriculum. In addition, teachers need to demonstrate full empathy and a sympathetic attitude when encountering minority students. The purpose of equity pedagogy is to equip students to respond with positive actions to make a better society that serves the interests of all people, especially those who are largely discriminated against.

Initiating Inquiry

Equity pedagogy teachers need to be critical analysts in order to facilitate student learning in and out of the classroom. They should incorporate a critical approach to their own teaching to increase equity among social groups.[55] Teachers need to examine sociocultural factors that affect education by promoting democratic classrooms, encouraging critical reflection, critiquing structural inequality, and advocating for social change. To this end, teachers criticize the function of schooling as a social reproduction agent, which might perpetuate the existing social structure, before setting up an educational intervention for social justice. Freire[56] encourages teach-

---

53. Nieto and Body, *School Reform.*
54. Picower, *Using Their Words.*
55. Picower, *School Reform.*
56. Freire, *Teachers as Cultural Workers.*

ers to use three analyzing skill sets when facilitating a lesson for social justice and equity: 1) problem posing, 2) codification, and 3) conscientization.

First, the teacher asks questions that help students identify problems facing their community. The teacher works with their students to discover ideas or create symbols (representations) that explain their life experiences (codification). By bracketing experiences, students engaged in the process can contextualize their experience and begin to see how they themselves act while actually experiencing the situation they are now analyzing, and thus reach a perception of their previous perception. By achieving this awareness, they come to perceive reality differently. This process provides insight for an individual and for society and also transforms a school into a more participative and collaborative setting where all children can share, develop, and create learning opportunities together. This is called "conscientization," which means that the teacher encourages analysis of prior experiences and of society through reflection and action.

Nurturing SEL

Can the current social emotional learning framework function positively to promote educational equity and justice? Unfortunately, current models of SEL can center white and middle-class knowledge systems as superior to all others, positioning marginalized students as incompetent and/or troubled, and ultimately perpetuate injustices.[57] In order to sustain social-emotional learning for marginalized and minority students, teachers need to build a healing school environment that practices restorative justice, where students freely share and discuss the issues of oppression, racism, and social injustice. This environment should be aligned through school policy, programs, and curriculum.[58] Strong and MaMain posit this kind of environment:

> Rather than "weighing" students' experiences against one another, students should be able to express their range of social and emotional needs without fear of judgment. Educators must also help students recognize how their individual experiences are tethered to larger systems. To be compassionate members of a community, students must understand how injustices are produced through

57. Strong and McMain, *Social Justice Learning*.
58. Dillard, *You Are Because I Am*.

systems, not just individuals, and how they themselves are implicated in these systems.[59]

The best strategy to implement equity-oriented social-emotional
learning is to create a covenant statement. Students may discuss the agree-
ments or promises that they have made that operate fundamentally with
racism and all the other injustices of power at the school.[60]

Gaining Community Actualization

The effectiveness of Jesus' teaching led to great success. The marginalized
woman was restored to her life, switching from loneliness to community,
and she immediately ran to her village to spread the truth. She totally actualized herself as an agent to transform the community. Note that Jesus'
blessing to the woman of Samaria spread to others. Similarly, spiritual care
directed toward the person who is disabled can spill over to their immediate and extended family, even to their community. She used to isolate
herself from her community; however, now she actively involved herself in
the community in collaboration and teamwork.

As I mentioned in the previous chapter (chapter 9), the current education system focuses too much on a student's personal well-being and
individual academic achievement. However, we need to cultivate a com-
munity-oriented, relationship-centered education paradigm in which we
practice valuing a better society together.

We need to teach students how to analyze institutional inequality in
their own life circumstances by allowing them to engage in social action
so they can change unfair social processes. Bridges are built between various oppressed groups so they can work together to advance their common
interests. Yes, teachers should implement strategies individually and col-
lectively to create equitable classrooms for all students regardless of their
social standing in society.

CONCLUDING REMARKS

The issue of educational equity should be seriously considered so that social justice is at the core of curriculum in schools. The learning process

59. Strong and MaMain, *Social Justice Learning*, 6.
60. Dillard, *You Are Because I Am*.

should be an intentional intervention where educational and social inequality and unjust treatment are removed. Students should be aware of the injustice found in society and learn how to acquire constructive responses. Throughout education and schooling, teachers may facilitate three pathways of change for social action that focus on education: 1) the transformation of self, 2) the transformation of schools and schooling, and (3) the transformation of society.[61]

61. Gorski, *Multicultural Education*.

11

Thriveology and Resilience-Informed Lesson Planning and Teaching

The disciples went and woke him, saying "Master, Master, we're going to drown!" He got up and rebuked the wind and the raging waters; the storm subsided and all was calm.

(LUKE 8:24)

INTRODUCTION

Trauma is an unexpected yet inevitable part of human life. Jesus said blessed are the poor in spirit, those who mourn, those who hunger and thirst, etc. So far, I have introduced eight different resilience-informed cases based on Matthew 5:3–12. Here, I will culminate each of the six stages of CARING with specific strategies to effectively teach students who experience trauma. This chapter consists of three parts. First, I will explain the teaching strategies of Jesus to his disciples who experienced trauma. Then, I will identify his teaching strategies in a resilience-informed lesson. Finally, I will illustrate a resilience-informed lesson plan.

WHEN THE DISCIPLES OF JESUS EXPERIENCED TRAUMA (LUKE 8:22–25)

One day, Jesus asked his disciples to cross over the sea in a boat. While the boat was making its way across the sea, the weather suddenly changed; a storm came on and nearly drowned the boat. The waves filled the boat so that it tossed up to the top of the billows, then sunk down to the bottom of the deep. The disciples desperately worked to pour the water back into the sea, but the boat was on the brink of perishing. They woke up Jesus, who had fallen asleep. Full of despair and fear, they shouted for help with loud voices, "Master, Master, we are going to drown" (Luke 8:24). In the same situation, Mark 4:38 states that they said, "Teacher don't you care if we drown?" What did Jesus do? He got up and rebuked the wind and the raging waters. The results? The storm subsided and all was calm. Then he asked the disciples, "Where is your faith?"

We can infer several insightful strategies through this trauma-induced event on how to handle the trauma demonstrated by Jesus, the teacher. First, we learn that everyone can experience a storm (trauma) unexpectedly. The word in Greek here for "storm" is *seismos*, which means a terrible disaster (like COVID-19), or a sudden and deadly tempest (like earthquakes). As the disciples experienced an unexpected storm, we also may confront trauma without warning. The storm was so strong that the disciples, who had spent their lives fishing as seasoned fishermen, could not help but panic. When students experience trauma, they may be hopeless and completely demotivated.

One question that comes to mind whenever I read this story is: Did Jesus know the storm would come before he rode in the boat? Is that the reason why he slept peacefully on the stern? I don't know the answer, but one thing I know is that Jesus knew the direction and purpose of the journey. His disciples were afraid to drown, while Jesus pointed out the place where they should go. Before they rode in the boat, he said, "Let us go over to the other side of the lake" (Luke 8:22). Jesus reminded his disciples of the direction they should go at the beginning of the class, so that they would remember the place to which they were heading.

Another question I raise is: Why didn't Jesus warn his disciples of the storm in advance? The answer is empowerment. He empowered his disciples to handle the storm. This is a vital strategy when teaching traumatized students. Experiencing a trauma renders students powerless and helpless. Teachers may offer students tasks in order to gain confidence.

Jesus knew that his disciples had been fishermen for their living in the Sea of Galilee. He trusted them to handle the situation. That's why, I think, Jesus slept calmly. He seemed to have been unaware and unconcerned when a furious storm swept over the boat and his disciples tried their best to save themselves.

The disciples could not handle the storm and woke up Jesus for help. The teacher was their ultimate hope. This is called the "power of proximity" and a "personal anchor."[1] Students who have experienced trauma can calm themselves when they have a stable, positive relationship with at least one trusted adult who is with them at critical moments. Proximity leads to transformation, which changes their perspective to regain energy and focus. Establishing stable, positive, and emotional relationships with a traumatized student allows them to see things beyond their current trauma.

Jesus calmed down the storm, then asked the disciples, "Where is your faith?" Remember the order in which Jesus acted. He cleared all traumatic situations first, and then taught the disciples about their fear and lack of faith. In the midst of a storm (trauma), teachers must help students first before rebuking or teaching. Remember the order. Help first and then teach.

We can identify several principles of a resilience-informed lesson based on this story. In this class, Jesus was a teacher. The disciples in the boat were students who experienced trauma. The boat represents the classroom, while the rough sea and wind are symbols for the trauma that comes to students unexpectedly. The first principle is: do not rebuke students who are experiencing trauma; rather, gently recommend and encourage. Trauma is an experience that allows powerful and dangerous events to overwhelm a student's capacity to cope.[2] Like the disciples, the first response when students experience a trauma is fear. Embracing their feelings and emotions must take precedence before teaching them.

Second, teachers must empower students. As I mentioned, trauma reduces students' confidence in their lives, seeing their futures as negative, which produces depression, rage, and disregard for human life, theirs and others.[3] So, the purpose of a resilience-informed lesson is to promote students' resilience by which they regain self-efficacy to see their future positively, even acknowledging the difficulties alongside it. In order to do that,

1. Garbarino, "Educating Children."
2. Souers and Hall, *Fostering Resilient Learners*, 15.
3. Garbarino, "Educating Children."

teachers allow traumatized students opportunities to practice enjoyment in life and stress-coping strategies.

The final principle for teachers is "a guide on the side rather than a sage on the stage." Teachers are not recommended to direct, command, and lead all learning activities (teacher-centered pedagogy), but they may guide students on the side by enthralling students, engaging, and motivating them (student-centered pedagogy).

RESILIENCE-INFORMED CARING LESSON

In this book, I addressed the importance of thriving, not surviving, in spite of confronting trauma. Then, I explained the effective strategies of a resilience-informed lesson; then I identified eight different student cases who experience trauma along with appropriate teaching strategies that teachers might use in their class. In this section, I will culminate effective strategies of a resilience-informed lesson based on the six phases of the CARING process and share a sample lesson plan in the last section of this chapter.

Cultivating Connections

Making connections is the foundation upon which all learning happens. Students are motivated to learn when teachers connect the learning topic with a certain context familiar to students. This is also called a "teachable moment," and offers powerful opportunities for the brain to register knowledge enhanced by emotional responses for students of all ages.[4] Teachers can make connections using a variety of ways, materials, and learning contexts. Ballenger[5] calls it "puzzling moments," which are known for being unplanned and surprising happenstances of learning.

Edmund Hansen[6] identifies four conditions through which teachers can cultivate connections with students effectively: 1) a systematic treatment of typical student misconceptions about the discipline and about research in general, 2) the promotion of personal academic interests, 3) attention to skill building, and 4) an emphasis on critical reflection and self-assessment.

---

4. Willis, *Teachable Moments*.
5. Ballenger, *Puzzling Moments, Teachable Moments*.
6. Hansen, *Creating Teachable Moments*, 8.

How may we create teachable moments and make them last? What are effective strategies for teachers to cultivate connections with students? First, teachers must improve their sensibility to know when to enact a teachable moment. Teachers must get to know their students' interests, hobbies, and personal and cultural backgrounds in order to connect with them when they teach. Teachers must develop unique capacities in order to promote students' curiosity and puzzlement, through which all students may fully and enthusiastically engage in learning activities and processes.[7]

Second, teachers need to prepare and develop repertoires for cultivating connections with students at any time and with any topic if necessary.[8] The table below is a summary of the four ways teachers can cultivate useful connections with students.

Table 11.1: **Four Ways of Cultivating Connections**

Physical connection	Using specific resources, materials, objects, facilities, place, visuals, social media/technology, newspaper, books, articles, manipulatives that related to the topic which will be taught
Psychological connection	Connecting the learning topics with student's situation, context, cultural/linguistic background, fund of knowledge, humorous ideas, interests, needs, and assets
Cognitive connection	Relating the lesson topic with students' worldview, perspective, misconceptions/stereotypes/myths/blind spots/overgeneralizations about the discipline/issues; conflicts; emphasis on critical reflection and self-assessment; attention to skill building; philosophical and historical questions
Symbolic connecting	Using abstract concepts using symbols, images, emblems, logos; humility and servanthood; greatness is serving

Lastly, teachers need to know students' developmental stages and developmental tasks. Students' physical, social, moral, cognitive, as well

---

7. Ballenger, *Puzzling Moments, Teachable Moments.*

8. Sapon-Shevin, *Teachable Moments*

as spiritual developmental stages and key tasks need to be remembered in order to create effective connections with them.

Affirming Personhood

There are many students in the classroom who are marginalized and treated unfairly due to physical, ethnic, gender, religion, and disability differences. However, all students can learn and be successful in education if teachers build a safe and comfortable learning climate where their students are respected and valued. Yes, affirming each student's personhood is critical. Building a positive and stable self-concept is the most important relationship of all. When a student's relationship with him/herself is toxic, he/she relates the similar pattern of relationships with others. Students' self-concept can be promoted by teachers confirming their value and dignity.

How do teachers affirm students' personhood in the midst of trauma and difficulties in their lives? First, as Nieto[9] clearly posits, teach by stimulating the full range of their personhood so that each student constructs a self that is worthy of respect and esteem. Teachers may set high expectations for all students in which all learning goals will be met via rich and differentiated instructional strategies. Positive responses of teachers to their students, particularly in the form of praise, encouragement, and support, constitute an affirmation of students' personhood and are vitally necessary for continued growth and accomplishment.

In addition, teachers must build a trusting relationship where all students freely and actively express their interests, skills, and strengths. Education is a focused and intentional process reflecting an understanding of all students as having talents and strengths that are fully utilized and incorporated in educational experiences. Simultaneously establishing a fair and equitable classroom culture is critical. Teachers need to get rid of any kind of prejudice, stereotype, and discrimination toward specific races, genders, cultures, and religions both in and out of the classroom.

In order to affirm each student's personhood, I recommend that teachers incorporate a strength-based educational approach and character education in their teaching and classroom management strategies. Strength-based education emphasizes the positive aspects of student effort and achievement as well as human strengths.[10] It is a drastic change in the

9. Nieto, *Identity, Personhood*.

10. Lopez and Louis, *Principles of Strengths-Based Education*.

educational paradigm to shift from viewing students and learning from a needs-based remediation approach to a strengths-based growth approach. The table below is a brief summary of each paradigm.

Table 11.2: The Difference between Needs-Based Remediation vs. Strengths-Based Growth Approaches

Needs-Based Remediation Approach	Strengths-Based Growth Approach
Usually used to identify gaps between students' desired and current level of achievement and to screen for deficits,	Promotes student's confidence by focusing on students' strengths, talents, and assets;
Focuses on students' past failures and deficiencies,	Views students as resourceful and resilient in the face of adversity;
Treat students as deficient to be filled, by viewing students as demoralized, stigmatized, which reduces student motivation,	Increases personal and academic confidence and promotes motivation to achieve the learning goals;
Destroys student confidence, which lowers students' aspiration to achieve learning goals;	Promotes positive development and interpersonal relationships;
Used in traditional education settings and the mental health field.	Builds resilience and a growth mindset to confront challenges and difficulties;
	Based on positive psychology and learner-centered education.

A strengths-based approach begins with teachers discovering the strengths of each student, fostering their development and integrating their new behaviors associated with positive outcomes. It is a cyclic designing process that requires assessing, teaching, and monitoring activities to help students identify, develop, and apply their strengths into their learning process, as well as personal relationships, to levels of personal excellence.[11] In order to do that, teachers must do a universal screening process through which they systematically identify each student's strengths and assets at the beginning of the school year. Students' strengths will continually be developed throughout the year by incorporating and applying them in educational programs, extracurricular activities, as well as after school activities.

Character education is another critical approach to affirm students' personhood. Character education refers to programs designed to promote

11. Anderson, *What Is Strengths-Based Education?*

positive character development in students by fostering social-moral competency in their thoughts and actions.[12] How can teachers incorporate character education in their teaching? Lickona[13] recommends several classroom practices that teachers may implement: 1) teachers need to act as a caregiver by treating each student with love and respect; 2) teachers create a moral community and practice moral discipline; 3) teachers create a democratic classroom environment, involving students in the decision making process; 4) teachers instruct value through the curriculum, using ethically rich content of academic subjects; and 5) teachers use cooperative learning to develop students' appreciation of others, perspective taking, and ability to work with others toward common goals. Sheasley[14] also asks teachers to teach character traits such as friendship, perseverance, responsibility, respect, self-discipline, cultural sensitivity, and courage.

In this stage of affirming personhood, teachers must build an equitable and fair classroom environment. In order to do that, I recommend implementing four principles. First, make every student feel they belong to the classroom community. The principles of equity pedagogy, in which every student's personal value and strengths matter in every moment in and out of the classroom, should be implemented. Second, teachers must expect every student to succeed no matter what differences and challenges each student encounters or experiences. Teachers must express their conviction that all students can learn so that all students know it clearly. Third, teachers must make their teaching and management processes transparent. Teachers need to clearly and specifically communicate their expectations for assignments and academic tasks. This kind of transparency is essential to an equity-minded classroom in order to teach students who experience trauma, which may threaten their sense of physical and psychological safety. Lastly, teachers must work hard to build inclusive and culturally responsive classroom environments. Remember, a teacher is a cultural mediator. Teachers may use their students' cultures as a vehicle for learning, allowing them to use their home languages during discussions and class activities. Students are encouraged to bring and share their cultural artifacts and products. Teachers ensure that students discover personal meaning and deepen their cultural identity as well as their sense of dignity.

12. Rawana et al., *Application of a Strengths-Based Approach*, 128.
13. Lickona, *Return of Character Education*, 8–9.
14. Sheasley, *Building a School*.

Restoring Relationships

The previous stage, affirming personhood, is critical in confirming each student's personal value. This stage works to emphasize creating a reliable relationship with others. How can we build a positive relationship with each other in classes? Two relationship strategies may be considered: universal and selected relationship-building strategies. The former refers to strategies to help the most students in a class, while the latter refers to accommodations or differentiated strategies for students who experience trauma. Universal strategies are common ideas that are applicable to most classrooms, such as creating caring classroom climates, supporting positive peer interactions, promoting students' social emotional capacities, and teaching problem-solving, planning, and responsive decision-making skills.[15] Anderson, Blitz, and Saastamoinen[16] recommend implementing a positive behavioral model, "I do; we do; you do," when teaching new behavior or content, emphasizing positive relationships with students. Teachers provide specific and concrete feedback by establishing predictable and understandable routines.[17] Hansen[18] identifies a set of strategies to create relationships with students:

- Relate the course content to students' own lives or show how this content can make a different in real life.

- Provide opportunities for students to clarify their own values and beliefs on which they base their opinions and decision-making.

- Help students discover their personal strengths that can enable them to be successful in a field of study.

Selected relationship-building strategies is a customized intervention for students who may have different learning needs, such as traumatized students, minority students, and special education students. The purpose of employing selected relationship-building strategies is to empower and help students to have a successful school experience by building positive relationships with other students as well as with teachers. Students who experience trauma might hold negative feelings toward relationships, fueled by feelings of inadequacy and lack of trust. In addition, they are also

15. Greene, *Collaboration, Texts.*
16. Anderson et al., *Exploring a School-University Model.*
17. Minahan, *Resilience-Informed Teaching.*
18. Hansen, *Creating Teachable Moments,* 13–14.

at greater risk for being retraumatized during their school experience if it is not addressed effectively.[19] Pica-Smith and Scannell[20] suggest several strategies that help teachers to develop healthy relationships with students:

1. Recognize that students cannot decontextualize their learning from their social identities or the sociopolitical context.

2. Find ways to authentically connect with each student and have a willingness to be vulnerable by taking steps to learn students' names, understanding who they are in the context of their lives and learning the strengths that they are bringing to our classrooms.

3. Be prepared to play multiple roles and to be flexible. Teachers need to creatively and flexibly adapt the classroom situation in order to address students' specific needs.

4. Be clear and consistent in expectations and communication. Miscommunication and confusion of expectations can increase the stress experienced by students.

Haggis[21] proposes three components to support those students effectively: 1) building positive peer culture in which students offer each other acceptance and encouragement, 2) developing appropriate social skills, and 3) supporting and caring for students by adults in a school. Minahan[22] also recommends several interventions, such as promoting predictability and consistency and providing predictability through visual schedules of the class agenda or school day.

Finally, equipping students with social emotional capacities and building resilience is critical when teaching traumatized students because they may have a significant resistance to learning as a result of trauma's effects on their self-regulatory capacities and relational abilities. Stress reduction and relaxation techniques should also be included in class instruction. For example, students may identify their own stress and learn basic stress reduction techniques (such as deep breathing, stretching, muscle tense and release, etc.).

19. Gutierrez and Gutierrez, *Developing a Resilience-Informed Lens.*

20. Pica-Smith and Scannell, *Teaching and Learning,* 79–81.

21. Haggis, *Influencing Positive Outcomes.*

22. Minahan, *Resilience-Informed Teaching Strategies.*

Initiating Inquiry

In chapter 2, I explained the three approaches of inquiry-based learning: guided inquiry, discovery, and problem-based. These three approaches are dialogue-oriented, constructivism-based, and exploratory pedagogical models which can be effectively applicable to teach students, especially those who experience trauma and difficulties. Teachers can use each of these three approaches based on the complexity of learning tasks and the level of students' readiness. For example, if the learning task is at the low level of Bloom's taxonomy and students are not well equipped with critical thinking skills, teachers may use the guided inquiry approach. However, if students are fully equipped to handle high levels of cognitive capacities and are ready to tackle the real problems in collaborative ways, then teachers may use the problem-based learning approach.

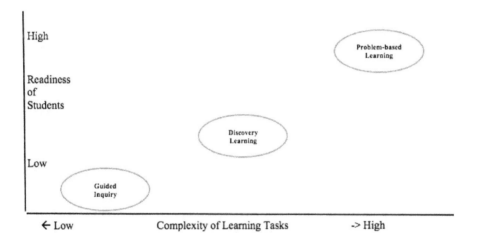

Figure 11.1: Three Approaches of Inquiry-Based Learning

The guided inquiry is a questioning pedagogical approach where teachers facilitate the learning with well-organized questions in order to inspire students' critical thinking. Teachers usually lead a lesson with open-ended, divergent questions to inspire students' critical and creative thinking skills through which students understand rules, concepts, and principles and gain new insights. A teacher guides the learning process at the side and encourages students to be the owner of their own learning process. Therefore, teachers' questioning skills (such as active listening, summarizing, paraphrasing, redirecting, clarifying, and structuring etc.) are critical to facilitate the inquiry process. The guided inquiry usually takes a three-step learning process: 1) begin with intriguing questions, 2) lead contextualized inquiry, and 3) allow students to explore new learning.[23]

Discovery learning is designed for students to achieve a deeper level of understanding new concepts, worldviews, values, and perspectives. Teachers present examples and the students work with them until they discover the interrelationships and learning takes place through inductive reasoning.[24] I explained discovery learning in the previous chapter.

In problem-based learning, students tackle authentic, ambiguous, open-ended problems that may have many potential solutions. This is the highest learner-centered approach in which students plan, organize, and evaluate the whole process by engaging the problem in teams.[25] The teacher's role in this approach is to model high-order thinking skills while probing for student understanding in order to solve the problem. In order to implement this approach, students need to be equipped with sound knowledge and skills to handle difficult problems or complicated issues. Students are encouraged to seek solutions for themselves by communicating with each other. Teamwork and collaboration are essential where they exchange ideas, articulate problems, and construct meanings.

In any approach a teacher may adopt, assessment is crucial. Teachers need to assess student learning against the lesson objectives. Teachers' formative and summative assessments are important, but I recommend the use of ongoing student self-assessments in which students monitor their own learning.

Nurturing SEL

Students who experience trauma may gradually lose hope, believing that they are incapable, suffering under stereotype threat.[26] In order to promote students' social and emotional capacities, there are several strategies that are applicable in the classroom. For example, Wilpow et al.[27] suggest the following strategies: 1) always empower and never disempower, 2) provide

23. Lee and Freeman, *Three Models of Constructivist Learning*.

24. Lee and Freeman, *Three Models of Constructivist Learning*.

25. Lee and Freeman, *Three Models of Constructivist Learning*.

26. Hammond, *Culturally Responsive Teaching*, 91.

27. Wilpow et al., *Heart of Learning*.

unconditional positive regard, 3) be a relational coach, and 4) provide guided opportunities for helpful participation.

In chapter 6, I explained the negative cycle with three stages: discouragement, learned helplessness, and internal oppression. They usually experience learned helplessness in which they believe that they have no control over their ability to improve their situation. Hammond[28] uses the term "internalized oppression" to explain traumatized students' inner situation in which they internalize the negative social messages about their current situations. It happens when a student becomes anxious about his inadequacy as a learner because he believes his failure on an assignment or test will confirm the negative stereotype associated with his race, socioeconomic status, gender, or language background. So, traumatized students easily give up confronting new environments or challenges. Therefore, the goal of SEL is to restore self-efficacy by building on students' social, cognitive, and emotional strengths as we help them continue to develop their competencies. Negative thoughts will change their brain wiring in a negative direction and throw their minds and bodies into stress.[29] But if people demonstrate a positive attitude, the good choice rewires everything back to the original, healthy, positive state.[30] Then students regain a sense of optimism and see their future positively, which finally leads to satisfaction with their lives.

As I mentioned in chapter 2, social-emotional learning concerns development in five capacities: self-awareness, self-management, social awareness, relationship skills, and responsible decision-making. In order to develop those five capacities, teachers need to focus on developing students' positive attitude, through which they will learn optimism, which eventually affects satisfaction with their life. Through all these processes, students will regain self-efficacy, which is the goal of social-emotional learning.

Sadly, much of the existing work has largely been focused on discrete programs; however, SEL competencies cannot be taught separately as a discrete program; rather, they must be implemented comprehensively throughout teaching and instruction, classroom management, and one-on-one conversation with each student, by allowing responsibility and choice, and by building warmth and support. Mehta[31] recommends four effective

28. Hammond, *Culturally Responsive Teaching*, 91.

29. Leaf, *Switch on Your Brain*.

30. Leaf, *Switch on Your Brain*, 36.

31. Mehta, *How Social and Emotional Learning*.

strategies on how SEL can succeed: 1) integrate academic and SEL learning, 2) avoid one-size-fits-all approaches, 3) stimulate demand but don't mandate, and 4) increase the supply of models and practical guidance. Sugishita and Dresser[32] propose to use SEL in two ways: as learner-centered instruction strategies (active engagement and equitable access) and learner-centered positive discipline strategies. The table below is the summary of these three types of SEL strategies that help teachers implement in their daily work.

Table 11.3: Three Types of SEL Strategies

SEL strategies	Specific strategies that teachers may integrate in their teaching
Active student engagement	Encourage students to stay on task and be more attentive and involved in the instruction; integrate into whole-class, small-group, and individualized learning; support competencies including responsible problem-solving, decision-making, communication/listening skills, and respectful relationship-building.
Equitable access to learning	Teachers provide appropriate scaffolds and accommodations so that students become confident; teachers draw from an arsenal of accommodations to meet the academic and socio-emotional needs and strengths of the diverse learners in their classrooms.
Positive and caring discipline strategies	Teachers convey care and support to students by using language that promotes students' self-confidence, motivation, and self-awareness.

How can teachers incorporate SEL in their teaching and discipline strategies? First, they must teach SEL systematically and clearly. Cartledge and Milburn[33] mention that SEL skills and concepts must be taught in three parts. They must be (1) taught explicitly, (2) performed frequently with feedback on the performance, and (3) generalized and transferred to other real-world situations. The five core competencies of socioemotional competencies (self-awareness, self-management, social awareness, relationship skills, and responsible decision-making) should be taught, practiced,

32. Sugishita and Dresser, *Social Emotional Learning*, 44–47.
33. Cartledge and Milburn, *Teaching Social Skills*.

and rehearsed every day in the classroom. Teachers may use the checklist to consider how they support and emotional learning for students.

Second, teachers' personal and relational support is critical. Osterman[34] proposed two roles that teachers should adopt: 1) academic support (teacher as instructional leader) and 2) personal support (teacher as a person). SEL capacities can be developed through academic practices using cooperative learning, classroom discussions, self-assessment, and reflective activities, etc. Personal support is fundamental, through which students are securely connected and attached with the teacher. In order to promote personal support effectively, consider how the following strategies may be effective:

- Know student names; greeting students; recognizing their strengths and gifts.

- Practice listening more than speaking. Listening communicates a sense of respect for and an interest in the student's contributions.[35]

- Give hugs, high fives, or pats on the shoulder. These can make a student feel safe and secure, and can help reduce their fear and distribute oxytocin throughout the body, causing stress reduction and increasing mood regulation.[36]

- Use more feeling words so that students can develop language to better verbalize their own emotions and begin to self-regulate their behavior.

Gaining Community Actualization: School a Change Agent

Education is an intentional activity through which students gain knowledge of themselves in relationship to others as well as nature. The Bible calls it *shalom*, which defines "the inner wholeness of the fulfilled person, but it is also a relational word including (upward) peace with God and (outward) peaceful integration within the society of God's people."[37] The Bible teaches that education exists to build the community of shalom, where all people and cultures are linked together in unity, contributing to society with their unique qualities that are developed in classrooms. However, traditional

34. Osterman, *Students' Need for Belonging.*
35. Hammond, *Culturally Responsive Teaching.*
36. Keown et al., *Creating a Community of Caring.*
37. Motyer, *Message of Philippians*, 209.

education has emphasized too much individual students' well-being and self-actualization under capitalistic influences. It is time to switch the educational focus to fulfill community actualization, contributing to our society and community better and healthier for all. The power of education is to make a positive impact on the community to make a better life and greater society for all.

How can we actualize the value of community in education? First of all, we need to build a collaborative school culture. Building a collaborative relationship with not only students and staff, but also with parents and community members, is critical. All stakeholders and their opinions must be valued in order to create a more equitable community at school. Janet Hansen[38] identifies three levels of organization in schools, individual, classroom, as well as school levels. In order to initiate school level change, she recommends developing positive school cultures, including collaborative planning, shared leadership, open communication, and support. Schools should confront issues of bias, prejudice, discrimination, and injustice, and implement efforts to reduce them and to build and manage diversity, equity, and social justice initiatives.

Second, instructional and academic, behavioral, as well as social-emotional interventions should be interconnected with each other to provide comprehensive supporting systems. Keown, Carroll, and Raisor[39] suggest several school-wide intervention strategies including a therapeutic toolbox and supportive peers. The former is designed to support students with multi-tiered school-wide support (MTSS), which gives them a safe place to talk about an experience, describe a fear, or relieve frustration, or simply provides a friendly face to say hello to everyday. Supportive peers proactively create plans that serve as guidelines to the kinds of interactions and activities that will benefit the student.

Finally, students' learning from their classrooms should be applied to their personal and community contexts by extending their thinking and transferring their knowledge to new situations. Therefore, school should be the change agent to transform the community and society by applying what students have learned from the classrooms. Yes, the school community would be a therapeutic, joyful learning space where students who have been traumatized may be healed and restored in a caring community. We need to

---

38. Hansen, *Managing Your Mindset*.
39. Keown et al., *Creating a Community of Caring*.

exert all our efforts to build our society to be a more equitable, democratic community where all students are respected and growing together.

CONCLUDING REMARKS

Education is our hope. Through education and schooling we can build a better society and greater world. We need to equip future generations with sound knowledge, appropriate skills, and responsible dispositions so that they make right decisions about social and community issues. Now it's time to focus on community actualization, committing to the ideals of democracy, equality, and justice for all students.

LESSON PLAN (EXAMPLE)

Below is an example of a simple lesson plan based on the CARING process. Teachers can add, modify, and revise when they teach their content areas.

Lesson Preparation	Create lesson objectives. The teacher may identify two lesson objectives: cognitive (content) as well as non-cognitive objectives. The latter one is an action that is taken with the objective of enhancing each student's self-efficacy and growth mindset through which they recognize their life positively. (For example, at the end of the class, students will confidently create a personalized plan of their choice to confront the trauma or adversity they experience.)
	Prepare learning resources and materials that would be related to students' real-life, day-to-day experiences. The teacher collects case studies of people who thrive and flourish in spite of confronting troubles and problems.
Cultivating Connections	The teacher begins the class by generating interest and encouraging students to join in the learning experiences. Anticipatory set based on the information of students' assets and needs, through music, visuals, drawing the class, which predict greater student attention and engrossment.
	Teachers may use people's stories who overcome their trauma and adversity and lead a discussion, identifying strategies on how to confront the challenges in the current contexts; to achieve these ends, students created a "my strengths tree," which identifies each student's assets and strengths on the form given.
	A good resource for the lesson is the KWL chart. Students can work individually or in a group. This helps students organize information before a unit or a lesson to engage them in a new topic/lesson by activating prior knowledge and sharing the lesson objectives.

Affirming Personhood	The teacher and students discuss classroom rules, procedures that emphasize respect for each other, help understand each other, investigate and determine how human rights are crucial and urgent.
	The teacher identifies each student's needs and assets, cultural, family backgrounds and contexts. The teacher may allow students to write "my story," sharing their contextual information as well as their interests, hobbies, and aspirations.
	The teacher may encourage students to study how effective people constantly broaden, modify, and strengthen their lifestyles and frame life events with a growth mindset.
	The teacher connects students' assets to curriculum, classroom activities, as well as their assignments.
Restoring Relationships	Establish and rehearse classroom rules, regulations, and procedures in which all students and their cultures are respected and valued.
	Teachers demonstrate their conviction that all students can learn and be successful in spite of differences in languages, cultures, and abilities in their teaching as well as classroom management strategies. They maintain positive and collaborative relationships between teacher and students (especially those who are experiencing trauma and difficulties) and among students.
	Teachers need to identify appropriate UDL (multiple means of representation, action/expression, engagement), differentiation (content, process and product), accommodation/ modification strategies based on the needs and assets of each student.
	Teachers allow students many opportunities in which each student's strengths and gifts are practiced and utilized so that students gain confidence from them.

Initiating Inquiry	The teacher may implement one of three modes of learner-centered pedagogy (guided inquiry, discovery and problem-based learnings) based on students' levels of readiness and the characteristics of learning tasks.
	Teachers clarify new concepts and terms such as oppression, domination, prejudice, bias, racism, democracy, equity etc., with key ideas and features contextually related the concepts to each student's sociocultural, historical context and personal background, using examples, counterexamples, stories, historical incidents, visuals, objects, etc.
	Dialogue is the center of the pedagogical process. Students and teachers are co-investigators in dialogue through which students enhance their critical consciousness of the power dynamics that have prevented them from fully realizing their humanity. Teachers help students to understand, investigate, and determine how implicit cultural assumptions, frames of reference, perspectives, and biases within a discipline influence the ways in which knowledge is constructed within it.
	In order to promote students' non-cognitive capacities, the teacher encourages students to study the lives of philosophers, novelists, musicians, poets, and inventors as incorporating their literature, poetry, play, music in the lesson.
	Teachers may provide a real problem (in a case study, project, assignment, or discussion topic) in which students tackle the task without the teacher's direct assistance. Teachers will check the process as well as the finished product.
	The teacher may choose an appropriate way of evaluation strategies. The assessment strategies should be congruent with two sets of objectives that were addressed in the first part of the lesson. Using the four levels of evaluation framework (I mentioned this in chapter 3), the application evaluation is crucial, in which teachers evaluate how far students have changed their behavior based on the learning they received. The lesson is not finished until students extend their learning into their practical situations.
	Assessment as learning is recommended, which encourages the use of student self-assessment by students in order to monitor their own learning.

Nurturing SEL	Teachers may modify their teaching in ways that will facilitate the academic achievement of students from diverse sociocultural, gender, and family-related backgrounds, using a variety of teaching styles and approaches that are consistent with the wide range of learning styles in various contexts.
	Teachers may create and practice routines so that students may follow them consistently and confidently (but sometimes being flexible for those who have different needs/contexts).
	Allow students empowerment by completing a task on their own and away from their teacher's guidance.
	The teacher may ask students to create a covenant statement (one example is addressed in chapter 10) in which they discuss agreements or promises about certain critical topics such as racism, injustice, prejudice, etc.
Gaining Community Actualization	Teacher always encourages the extension activity or task after teaching. This entails intentional efforts to extend learning beyond the classroom into relevant contexts in the real world. New behaviors must be congruent with the rest of the students' behaviors, personality, and environment. Students may participate in a certain project, community event, or specific assignment in order to promote social justice in and out of the classroom.
	All lessons learned can be extended to promote gender, racial, and social-class equality in a particular community students live in and a specific situation that students may confront. Students are highly recommended to participate in restructuring it by extending what they have learned.
	Emphasize students' personal as well as collaborative responsibility for what they have learned.
Reflection	Education is an iterative and cyclic process through which the teacher as well as students are advancing their journey, contributing to transform the society and community to be better.
	Education is an ongoing process in which the teacher reviews four stages (plan, teach and assess, reflect, and apply). In order to improve teaching, collecting and analyzing assessment data from students, stakeholders (parents, community, school administrator etc.), as well as the teacher him/herself would be crucial.

12

The GREAT Dispositions of a Resilience-Informed Teacher

Come with me by yourselves to a quiet place and get some rest.

(MARK 6:31)

INTRODUCTION

Jesus is known for his teaching. He is called "Teacher" forty-five times in the New Testament. Jesus called himself a teacher as well (Matthew 10:24; 23:8; Luke 6:40; John 13:14). His disciples and other followers called him a teacher as well. The Aramaic title *"Rabbi"* is used fourteen times to describe Jesus, even though he was not formally trained as a rabbi. However, people recognized him as a teacher and one-third of his ministry was devoted to teaching. He also proclaimed that his ministry was to teach in the temple court (Matthew 26:55). He was always surrounded by people steeped in traumatic and adverse situations, yet his teaching was impactful and transformative.

The success of resilience-informed teaching depends on the competencies of a teacher. What are the competencies of an effective resilience-informed teacher? In this chapter, I will address two issues. First, based on the Bible story in Mark 6 where Jesus fed the four thousand, I will identify the five roles of an effective resilience-informed teacher. Second, I will explain five dispositional competencies to demonstrate those five roles in their teaching and classroom management settings.

JESUS A GREAT TEACHER

One day, Jesus and his disciples were on their way to a quiet place to take a rest, but a large crowd followed Jesus. Jesus was compassionate because he saw them like sheep without a shepherd. The crowd was hungry, so Jesus' disciples found two fish and five loaves. Jesus gave thanks for the food, raised it to heaven, blessed it, and gave it to the disciples to distribute to the crowd. Everyone ate and was satisfied, and there was enough left over to fill twelve baskets. Based on this story (Mark 6), we can identify the characteristics of Jesus that can be applied to the classroom context. In this section, I identify the characteristics of Jesus as an effective teacher with five roles: a compassionate motivator, a warm demander, an effective caregiver, a contextual coach, and a problem-solver.

A Compassionate Motivator

Jesus was compassionate. Compassion, which is from the Greek root *splagchnizomai*, means to become close to the one who suffers by willing to become vulnerable oneself.[1] Compassion, therefore, means to suffer in order to enter fully into the situation of the other.[2] Mark 6:34 says, "When Jesus landed and saw a larger crowd, he had compassion on them, because they were like sheep without a shepherd." When Jesus saw them, he put himself in their places and understood their spiritual pains and sorrows because they did not have their shepherd. He wanted to comfort, encourage, and strengthen them, like a shepherd cares for his sheep safely and securely. Because he was a good shepherd who is compassionate (John 10), he laid down his life for his sheep. Scheffler[3] identifies characteristics of compassion based on the story of the Good Samaritan:

1. Compassion is experienced and expressed with regard to the suffering of others, not the self or the family.

---

1. Jonas, *Henri Nouwen*, 63.
2. MaAfee, *Unexpected News*, 112.
3. Scheffler, *Empathy*, 6.

2. Compassion is experienced with regard to serious suffering, not simple needs.

3. Compassion is generated by people imagining themselves in the predicament of the victims.

4. The compassion felt or rendered is unconditional; the victim most commonly is unaware of it and plays no conscious part in the onset of the compassion.

5. There occurs an identification with the victim, since the predicament is perceived as one's own possible fate.

6. The compassionate are willing to make sacrifices, to deny themselves pleasure in the action of care.

7. Compassion is not mere feeling, but is expressed in deeds of care.

8. Compassion is an overriding feeling that crosses national borders, recognizing the common human condition.

So what did Jesus, as the compassionate motivator, do? He taught many things (Mark 6:24). From a Christian standpoint, a shepherd is a teacher. As a shepherd leads the sheep by guiding, caring, and protecting, so a teacher in a classroom instructs, corrects, inspires, and facilitates students. How would a teacher be a compassionate motivator? First, compassion is an action-oriented affective state, in which teachers deeply emphasize with the emotions of students so that they can articulate their experience and receive care. Second, compassion leads to interaction with students, especially those who have been traumatized, mistreated, and oppressed physically, emotionally, and spiritually. Remember that Jesus' relations with stigmatized people were compassionate.[4] Like Jesus' compassion, teachers' hearts may go out to those students, so they know they are not alone, feeling their own sadness, anger, anxiety, and inadequacy. Demonstrating compassion toward students means providing restoring, healing, and reconciling broken relationships and gaining self-efficacy.

A Warm Demander

The disciples were shocked when Jesus asked them to feed the crowd. He said, "You give them something to eat" (Mark 6:37). However, they knew

4. McClure, *Introducing Jesus' Social Network*.

that it was impossible to do that because it may have required more than an eight-month wage (John 6:7). Of course, Jesus knew that his disciples couldn't solve this problem. Why then did he demand it? As I explained in the previous chapter (chapter 11), he empowered them to confront the situation, a key factor of resilience-informed teaching. The unique combination of personal warmth and active demandingness earns the teacher the right to push for excellence and stretch the student beyond his/her comfort zone.[5] Effective teaching is not to feed students with narrowly chopped content, but to empower them with a challenging task to deal with the problem. Though it takes time to challenge traumatized students to learn something new, eventually they will be changed through this process. The warm demander ultimately will help students take ownership of their learning to be more self-reflective and self-confident learners.

In order to be an effective warm demander, Safir[6] suggests four principles that teachers may implement in their classroom teaching. The table below is the summary of the four principles.

Table 12.1: Four Principles to Be a Warm Demander

Principles	Descriptions
Believe in the impossible	Every human being has the ability to grow and change.
Build trust	Warm demanders understand that all growth and learning is rooted in relational capital, the resource that leaders accrue when they take time to listen to and convey authentic care and curiosity toward others.
Teach self-discipline	A warm demander can communicate high expectations to his or her students and help them develop self-discipline.
Embrace failure	Warm demanders model a growth mindset toward their students and encourage a culture of experimentation.

---

5. Hammond, *Culturally Responsive Teaching*, 98.

6. Safir, *Becoming a Warm Demander*.

An Effective Caregiver

Helping others is an ongoing task without ceasing. Jesus' disciples were so burned out from their unstoppable teaching, preaching, and healing ministries with him. Mark 6:31 says that because so many people were coming and going, they did not even have a chance to eat, so he said to them, "Come with me by yourselves to a quiet place and get some rest." Jesus knew that his disciples needed a rest from their chronic exhaustion. Due to the ongoing teaching and support of students who have experienced trauma, teachers may acquire symptoms of compassion fatigue, such as interpersonal exhaustion, relational frustration, depression, diminished performance, and behavioral changes. As Jesus offered rest to his disciples, teachers also take care of their students' social-emotional stress. Furthermore, teachers need to maintain their own social and emotional well-being. How can teachers prevent possible compassion fatigue? Erdman, Colker, and Winter[7] suggest the following strategies in order to maintain holistic well-being.

- Physical needs: regularly eat nutritiously balanced meals, sleep adequately, exercise regularly.

- Social needs: cultivate and maintain close friendships.

- Mental health needs: do activities to keep your mind sharp, such as reading books or researching a topic you are interested in.

- Emotional needs: establish appropriate ways to process your emotions.

- Spiritual needs: nurturing your spirit involves doing things that bring meaning to your life.

A Contextual Coach

As I pointed out in the last chapter, the purpose of resilience-informed teaching is to equip traumatized students with a positive attitude and capacity for self-efficacy. In order to do that, teachers may allow opportunities through which students are empowered to handle tasks/assignments, to choose certain classroom activities or programs, and to decide their own learning agenda. That's why Jesus empowered his disciples by asking to give them something to eat in Mark 6. However, his disciples had no clue how to solve the situation. Though Jesus knew that they couldn't handle it,

7. Erdman et al., *Preventing Compassion Fatigue*, 32.

he coached and involved them in the problem-solving process. Mark 6:41 reads, "Then he gave them to his disciples to distribute to the people. He also divided the two fish among them all." Jesus was a coach, teacher, and mentor through which his disciples grew and matured cognitively as well as spiritually. Even though his disciples didn't meet his expectations, he never abandoned them or forsook them, but always gave them a second chance. Jesus demonstrated a typical example of a contextual coach who continues to trust his disciples, to involve them in his ministry by allowing them opportunities. He led an inquiry-based, discovery, and problem-solving lesson (as I explained in chapter 11) in which he coached their learning. After three years of ministry, his disciples were completely mature as enthusiastic and powerful characters due to his effective coaching.

Teachers' role as coach can be vital for those who experience trauma and stress. Students will be locked in a fight-flight-freeze mode if their stress and trauma are not safeguarded by a teacher (coach). When a teacher coaches traumatized students by building a safe and authentic relationship with them, students share their feelings and emotions freely, which causes the release of oxytocin, an anti-stress chemical.[8]

A Problem-Solver

Every student needs a success tutor from whom they learn how to solve their academic as well as social and relational problems. Demonstrating effective problem-solving processes regarding students' issues, especially those who experience trauma, is crucial to establish a sense of self-efficacy. Yes, a teacher should be a problem-solver. The final statement in Mark 6 is rather simple. It says, "They all ate and were satisfied" (Mark 6:43).

Since John Dewey identified the importance of a scientific problem-solving process in education, many theories have viewed teaching as a problem-solving process. The teacher as a problem-solver model identifies the stages of planning, designing, executing, and assessing to teach a math or science lesson effectively through which teachers continually reflect on effective methods to solve problems.[9] Think about the story in Mark 6. Jesus knew all situations very well: the needs of the crowd, using the resources to meet their needs, allocating his disciples to distribute to the crowd, etc. Like Jesus, teachers need to identify the needs and assets of students, collect

8. Hammond, *Culturally Responsive Teaching*.
9. Stuessy and Naizer, *Reflection and Problem Solving*.

and analyze relevant data, along with aligning them well based on students' readiness so that they can become problem-solvers.

THE GREAT TEACHER DISPOSITIONAL COMPETENCIES

I believe that teachers must lead effective education. Recruiting quality teachers who are equipped with sound knowledge, skills, and dispositions can bring about the bright future of this country. How do we identify the competencies of a quality teacher? Based on the five roles that are demonstrated by Jesus (a compassionate motivator, contextual coach, warm demander, effective caregiver, and problem-solver), I will suggest a set of teacher dispositional competencies in this section. In other words, how would those five roles of a teacher demonstrate in a resilience-informed classroom where traumatized students are present? Resilience-informed teachers may possess particular dispositions (such as attitudes, commitment, intrinsic motivation, and competencies) that make them stand out by demonstrating effective teaching strategies when they teach traumatized students. In order to answer this question, I identified five key dispositional competencies, which are called GREAT (Gentle, Relational, Empowering, Adaptable, Transforming) competencies. Each of the five competencies corresponds with five roles of a resilience-informed teacher I have mentioned. These five dispositional competencies are gentle, relational, empowering, adaptable, and transforming. The figure below shows the five roles and dispositions of a resilience-informed teacher.

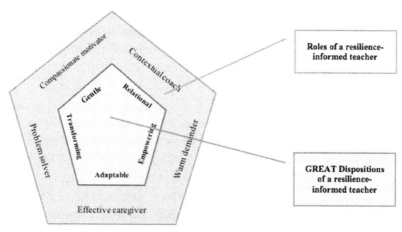

Figure 12.1: Roles and Dispositions of a Resilient-Informed Teacher

Be Gentle

The first disposition to be an effective resilience-informed teacher is gentleness.[10] This is about self-knowledge, asking who is the self that teaches, but is usually ignored by most teachers.[11] Why does answering this question matter? Because authentic and effective teaching usually comes from teachers' gentle hearts. Teacher's gentle spirit would be the foundation on which true education starts. Being gentle means the genuine, authentic love of their teaching, students, and teachers themselves. Being gentle refers to serving students and their communities willingly and sacrificially in and out of the classroom. Gentle teachers fully understand that teaching is a calling, vocation, and mission through which they leave a legacy to build an equitable and just society. A gentle teacher develops her professionalism throughout her life in order to serve students and the surrounding community with her expert knowledge and competencies. The gentleness of a teacher is the root of effective teaching for marginalized and traumatized students because their gentleness is built on safety, love, and engagement.[12]

How can we become this kind of a gentle teacher? How can we equip ourselves with gentleness? Practicing humility and humbleness is vital. Gentle teachers know that the power of education usually comes from inside of their hearts, alongside their sense of vocation, intellectual humility, their identity and integrity.[13] Parker Palmer[14] says that there are three sources of knowledge: curiosity, control, and love. A gentle teacher knows that only knowledge out of love, not curiosity or control, is the fundamental power that transforms their students. This attitude leads a gentle teacher to be intellectually humble, realizing that the purpose of knowledge is to serve students.[15]

---

10. I use the term "gentle" adopted from John McGee, *Gentle Teaching*, who created an approach for helping people with an intellectual disability, in which he establishes a framework to develop companionship, the unconditional relationship to educate students who experience stress. However, I use the term "gentle" a little bit differently in this chapter to refer to teacher's self-knowledge, understanding his/her own perspective on education, and teaching as a calling and vocation.

11. Palmer, *Courage to Teach*.

12. McGee and Brown, *Gentle Teaching Primer*.

13. Palmer, *Courage to Teach*.

14. Palmer, *To Know as We Are Known*.

15. Gould, *Outrageous Idea*.

Therefore, a gentle teacher practices vulnerability every day. People ask teachers to be omniscient and have a superman-like attitude and personality. However, gentle teachers recognize that they are mere human beings, and they are willing to let down their guard a bit. They offer their hurts and wounds to heal and comfort traumatized students' suffering and pain. A gentle teacher creates a culture of caring that both heals and is healed, shares and is shared, teaches and is taught.

Are you a gentle teacher? Are you willing to be? You may answer the following questions and evaluate your heart and check your perspectives.

- Do I know myself? Do I recognize my strengths as well as my weaknesses?

- What is the purpose of my teaching? Is teaching my passion and my vocation? Do I love teaching? Am I happy when I stand in front of my students?

- Do I love my students from the bottom of my heart? Do I want to spend time with my students in and out of the classroom to help them?

- Am I transparent? Do I hide myself from my students and others in fear of rejection from them?

- Are my public and private lives consistent? Am I the same person as before? Are my speech and deeds congruent?

Be Relational

The key issue of twenty-first-century education that contributes to successful education is building positive relationships.[16] Building a trusting and authentic relationship between teacher and students and between teacher and parents is a foundational factor for effective education where students are actively participating, engaging, and sharing with each other. True education starts only when the teacher relates to students through the dialogue with one another through which the teacher inspires students' critical and creative thinking skills. Thus, the second disposition of an effective resilience-informed teacher would be relational, a capacity for connectedness with students. Building relationships says to students that their teachers are interested in them, and this has an incredible power to motivate

16. Leadbeater, *It's All About Relationships*.

and facilitate powerful learning in a connected community.[17] Teachers' capacity to build relationships would be in three ways: building a positive relationship between teacher and students, among students, and between subjects and their students so that students can learn to weave a world for themselves.[18]

First, teachers must build a positive relationship with students in order for learning to take place. I addressed in the previous chapters many effective strategies to make positive relationships with students; however, the key would be "specific," "consistent," and "empathetic."[19] In addition, teachers need to listen to students more and speak less because the most powerful way to build rapport is by practicing listening.[20]

Second, building relationships between/among students themselves would be another critical teacher's capacity. According to research, the relationship between/among students is more important than the relationship between teacher and students. For example, when students perceive that they are accepted by fellow students, there is improvement in their psychological well-being.[21] Harmonious classrooms are marked by many warm and supportive relationships among students and few problematic relationships. Teachers need to promote students' relationship with trusted and reliable people; however, teachers need to prune and limit certain relationships and interactions with students who drain or deplete traumatized students.[22]

Third, building relationships between students and the contents and subjects they are studying would be another area that teachers need to care for. Teachers may weave the class using diverse methods and strategies such as Socratic dialogues, collaborative problem-solving, creative chaos, inquiry, exploratory pedagogy etc., where students ask questions, explore implications to their real-life settings, consider examples, test assumptions, and discuss how new ideas might apply in different situations.[23] When teachers create an effective lesson, students will be enthusiastically engaged

---

17. Martin, *Five Finger Challenge*.
18. Palmer, *Courage to Teach*.
19. Minahan, *Resilience-Informed Teaching Strategies*.
20. Hammond, *Culturally Responsive Teaching*.
21. McElhaney et al., *They Like Me*.
22. Fagell, *Coping with Change*.
23. McEwan et al., *Cultivating Hope through Learning*.

in the class activities by relating with each other, by connecting the content to their real-life situations.

Am I a relational teacher? Think about the questions below and assess your disposition as a relational teacher.

- Do I accurately read the verbal and nonverbal communication of students? Do I communicate with students with warmth and empathy?

- Do I know each of my student's interests, learning profiles, readiness, assets and needs, and family and cultural backgrounds?

- Do I create connections to subject matter that are meaningful to students?

- Do I foster relationships with students using specific, consistent strategies every day continually (for example, greeting students by name every morning at the door and making face-to-face contact with everyone in each class)?

- Do I communicate effectively with students, parents, and colleagues regularly and consistently?

Empowering and Equipping Students to Succeed

As I mentioned before, students who experience trauma and difficulty lose confidence and lack trying to challenge new things. Thus, teachers may offer small opportunities in which they may get through and gain little sense of accomplishment. Yes, empowerment is an essential strategy in trauma-sensitive teaching. Empowerment is defined as "a process whereby students develop the competence to take charge of their own growth and resolve their own problems."[24] That's why Jesus told his disciples, "You give them something to eat" (Mark 6:35–37). By saying that, Jesus imparted a vision that only he could see, and he also delegated the task to his followers to accomplish it at hand. Finally, he allowed them to share fully in the fulfillment of the vision.[25] The same thing happens to teachers when they teach traumatized students. Wolpow et al.[26] clearly suggests resilience-informed teachers always empower, never disempower. Classroom discipline may be

24. Short et al., *Creating Empowered Schools*, 38.
25. Briner and Prichard, *Leadership Lessons of Jesus*, 96.
26. Wilpow et al., *Heart of Learning*.

necessary, but it should be done in a way that is respectful, consistent, and nonviolent.

How can teachers promote students' sense of empowerment? McGee and Brown[27] suggest applicable strategies such as:

- Helping students become active participants as possible in their own lives;

- Entering into a student's space without the provocation of fear and with the evocation of a sense of peace;

- Avoiding expectations of compliance or blind obedience;

- Preventing physical, developmental, and emotional harm;

- Assuring active participation.

Teachers must allow students to fail, to commit mistakes. When traumatized students make an error on a class project, they may become easily frustrated and want to quit their work. However, they are less likely to do so if teachers tolerate mistakes, encouraging them with warm feedback. Teachers may use an empathetic approach by validating a student's feeling so that it avoids triggering a trauma response in the student.[28]

In order to promote a sense of empowerment, one strategy would be to allow them to spell out simple behavioral expectations. For example, students make a pledge in writing to learn something like, "I will maintain 95 percent daily attendance." or "I will be prepared for and participate and achieve in every class."[29] Finally, celebrate what students achieve, even a minor thing they complete, in order for them to regain their self-confidence. Teachers need to intentionally call attention to the positive effort and outcomes of what they have accomplished.

Am I an empowering teacher? You may think about the questions below and evaluate yourself.

- Am I a micromanager, controlling students in every detail? Or do I allow a space for students where they are responsible to do their work?

- Do I give students decision-making power in some areas of curriculum or classroom activities?

---

27. McGee and Brown, *Gentle Teaching Primer*, 14.

28. Minahan, *Trauma-Informed Teaching Strategies*.

29. Lamperes, *Empowering At-Risk Students*.

- Do I hear students' voices through forums, in-person conversation, and in-class discussion?

- Do I honor students' commitment? Do I accept students' ideas and opinions in teaching and other class activities?

- Am I a teacher who praises what students have accomplished or who usually criticizes how they are wrong? Do I see more of the positive side of my students than the negative side of my students?

Be Adaptable

When students experience trauma, they might feel like they can't control the environment and their own lives, so teachers can minimize the impact of loss of control by prioritizing what's most important and removing all other barriers. Newhouse[30] emphasizes flexibility as a vital priority in a resilience-informed learning. Teachers need to consider many factors that traumatized students bring to the classroom, evaluating all factors and adjusting all contexts to meet the needs of the student, which are the factors of effective teaching. Christenbury[31] defines it as contextual, which responds to individual students, school and classroom communities, and societal needs. Yes, teachers alter, adjust, and change their instruction depending on who is in the classroom and the extent to which those students are achieving.

Nodding[32] asks teachers to consider students' situation and context first by providing the welfare of students, acting in a non-rule-bound fashion. Instead of applying rigid standards and strict classroom routines to traumatized students, teachers may be flexible and adaptable when using the class rules for those students. There are clear lesson objectives and goals, yet there are diverse ways to get the goals, considering each student's context and situation at his own pace.

Thus, teachers may utilize various methods for students, flexible assignment deadlines, different ways of expression, giving students options, and developing personal agenda, etc. There are many strategies to address diverse students' needs using differentiated instruction, UDL,

30. Newhouse, *Four Core Priorities.*
31. Christenbury, *Flexible Teacher.*
32. Nodding, *Caring.*

accommodation, and modification, through which teachers provide appropriate support systems to alleviate students' stress and difficulties. Teachers should remember that students are infinitely more important than the subject. In order to do that, teachers may communicate frequently with students to get a sense of their evolving needs. Ziegler[33] suggests several ideas to help traumatized students using flexible teaching and classroom management strategies, including: teaching to the student's individual learning style, using a variety of activities and help with transitions, taking choices in areas of the students' interests, and employing cooperative group efforts that promote teamwork.

Am I an adaptable teacher? You may answer the questions below and reflect on your teaching style and evaluate yourself.

- Am I willing to adjust the lesson plans based on a student's specific situation and particular context?

- Do I respect the cultures of all students and am I sensitive to cultural norms? Am I open to learning different cultural facts and skills?

- Do I frequently talk with students and ask questions instead of making my personal assumptions?

- Do I arrange the classroom differently to meet traumatized students' different needs, such as using dimmed lights, cozy corners, warm colors, and flexible seating?

- Am I willing to receive constructive feedback in my teaching from my students as well as their parents and communities? Do I learn about students and their communities regularly?

Be Transformational

Education is a hope-filled endeavor by teachers to instill the value of justice, equity, and democracy in the lives of individual students and their communities. Teachers are difference-makers who empower students to actively engage with the opportunities and challenges that confront contemporary society and contribute in meaningful ways to the common good.[34] Therefore, the purpose of education is for students to apply what

---

33. Ziegler, *Optimum Learning Environment.*
34. McEwen et al., *Cultivating Hope through Learning.*

they have learned in the classroom to their personal lives as well as to their communities. I explained the framework of four levels of evaluation in chapter 3, where the effectiveness of education can be assessed on students' changed behavior (level 3 evaluation) and the impact to their organizations (level 4 evaluation). How can teachers facilitate learning to lead social change and transformation? James Banks[35] identifies education as a social action in which a teacher dedicates his/herself to continuously expanding her or his knowledge base through the exploration of various sources from various perspectives, and sharing that knowledge with her or his students. The voices of students regarding racism, sexism, injustice, prejudice, and bias are brought into the classroom and identify interventions in order to confront those issues appropriately in and out of the classroom settings. Freire[36] believes that education can be a strong weapon to accomplish the goal for liberation. In order to do that, he challenges teachers to become a "watchdog" on behalf of students, because teachers are the position to influence the way the students interpret the world around them. How can teachers lead an educational reform? Palmer[37] suggests four stages of school change:

- Stage 1: Isolated individuals (teachers) make an inward decision to live "*divided no more*," finding a center for their lives outside of institutions.

- Stage 2: These individuals begin to discover one another and form *communities of congruence* that offer mutual support and opportunities to develop a shared vision.

- Stage 3: These communities start *going public*, learning to convert their private concerns into the public issues they are and receiving vital critiques in the process.

- Stage 4: A system of alternative rewards emerges to sustain the movement's vision and to put pressure for change on the standard institutional reward system.

Learning is not simply an activity in which to engage for the sake of personal reward or personal satisfaction; rather it is a reformational intervention in which all people work together to fulfill a God-designed purpose

35. J. Banks, *Introduction to Multicultural Education*.
36. Freire, *Pedagogy of the Oppressed*.
37. Palmer, *Courage to Teach*, 172–73.

and function.[38] Teachers should be the agents to lead the educational change. How to be a transforming teacher? Are you that kind of teacher? You may answer the questions below and evaluate yourself.

- Am I incorporating students' real-life issues in my curriculum and lesson plans, allowing students to discuss them along with ideas to handle them appropriately?

- Am I longing for a society where all people are valued and respected? Am I pursuing the values of social justice, equity, and equality in my teaching and out-of-the-classroom extracurricular activities?

- Am I involved in a community or organizational activity that is designed to create a better society?

- Do I want to know what's going on in my school or community and discuss it with other people regularly and how to confront it?

- Am I willing to be a volunteer (or mentor) to help students learn better who have different learning needs such as ELs, special education students, students from poverty, and students who experience trauma and adversity?

Evaluate Your Dispositional Score

In this chapter, I have identified five roles of a resilient-informed teacher and five dispositional factors to perform each of five roles effectively. I hope teachers are equipped with these five dispositional capacities in order to make a positive impact on students' lives who experience trauma and adversity. Teachers may assess five dispositions based on the questions that I provided at the end of each section based on the 1–5 Likert scale (1 being very low and 5 being very high) and identify the areas of strength and weakness. Then you may create strategies to improve the weak area of disposition. I hope each of you will be a gentle, relational, empowering, adaptable, and transforming teacher.

---

38. McEwen et al., *Cultivating Hope through Learning.*

CONCLUDING REMARKS

"Be perfect, therefore, as your heavenly Father is perfect" (Matthew 5:48). Jesus asks us (teachers) to be perfect. The Greek word for "perfect" is *teleios*, which means complete in labor, mature, the final purpose toward which we are moving. Teachers are perfect when they are demonstrating their expertise and dispositions in full to touch as many students' hearts so that all students are fully developed with their potential gifts and talents. Teachers are perfect when they continue their educational journey in the right direction as God provides. Teachers are perfect as long as they are a compassionate motivator, contextual coach, warm demander, effective caregiver, and a problem-solver. As long as the teacher is effective, our society will be prosperous and the future of this country will be bright.

Epilogue

I BELIEVE THAT THE power of education lies in its therapeutic and reconciliatory purposes. Education brings healing to those who experience wounds from trauma and adversity. It also brings a shalom that liberates us from unjust practices (i.e., racism, bullying, prejudice, bias, ableism, ageism). It provides a learning environment that hears students' painful stories, identifies their symptoms, and offers relevant interventions as we pursue justice together.

In order to implement effective, therapeutic teaching in and out of classroom settings, I recommend that teachers reflect upon two themes. First, think about your teaching process, asking yourself, how would Jesus teach? If Jesus were to teach your class, how would he teach differently? In this book, I suggest the CARING model to guide teachers in implementing resilience-informed teaching in their classroom contexts.

Second, reflect upon your mindset regarding education. Education is a bidirectional process. The term "education" means to draw out something that students already possess. God created each student with full potential for knowledge, skills, and dispositions. Education is not a robotic process where teachers copy and paste their knowledge onto their students. Rather, it is a community-forming process between teacher and students. Education is an act of love; therefore, teaching is a demonstration of love. Racism, prejudice, myth, bias, and injustice begin with a lack of love. If a teacher loves students, s/he accepts students as they are, not considering the difference of each student's language, SES, skin color, or religion as a deficiency. Love builds a community of shalom, where all students develop with wholeness, soundness, health, safety, and prosperity at the horizon. Paul clearly defines the characteristics of love in 1 Corinthians 13:4–8, but I have switched "love" to "teaching" because it depicts the characteristics of teaching as well.

Teaching is patient, teaching is kind. Teaching does not envy, teaching does not boast, teaching is not proud. Teaching does not dishonor others, teaching is not self-seeking, teaching is not easily angered, teaching keeps no record of wrongs. Teaching does not delight in evil but rejoices with the truth. Teaching always protects, always trusts, always hopes, always perseveres.

Yes, teaching never fails. That's why Paul recommends us to keep going in Galatians 6:9, which reads, "Let us not become weary in doing good, for at the proper time we will reap a harvest if we do not give up."

Shalom,
HKL

Bibliography

Adams, Maurianne. "Social Justice Education." In *The Encyclopedia of Peace Psychology*, edited by Daniel J. Christie, 1033–36. Malden, MA: Wiley-Blackwell, 2010.

Adelman, Howard S., and Lynnett Taylor. "Classroom Climate." In *Encyclopedia of School Psychology*, edited by Steve W. Lee et al., 819–28. Thousand Oaks, CA: Sage, 2005.

Allport, Gordon W. *The Nature of Prejudice*. 25th anniversary ed. Boston: AddisonWesley, 1979.

Anderson, David. W. *Reaching Out and Bringing In: Ministry to and with Persons with Disabilities*. Bloomington, IN: WestBow, 2013.

Anderson, Edward. C. "What Is Strengths-Based Education?" 2004. https://www.weber.edu/WSUImages/leadership/docs/sq/strengths-base-ed.pdf.

Anderson, Elizabeth, et al. "Exploring a School-University Model for Professional Development with Classroom Staff: Teaching Trauma-Informed Approaches." *School Community Journal* 25:2 (Fall 2015) 113–34.

Apple, Michael. *Education and Power*. Boston: Routledge and Kegan Paul, 1982.

Assor, Avi, et al. "Choice Is Good, but Relevance Is Excellent: Autonomy-Enhancing and Suppressing Teacher Behaviors Predicting Students' Engagement in Schoolwork." *British Journal of Educational Psychology* 72:2 (2002) 261–78.

Ballenger, Cynthia. *Puzzling Moments, Teachable Moments: Practicing Teacher Research in Urban Classrooms*. New York: Teachers College, 2009.

Bandura, Albert. "Cultivate Self-Efficacy for Personal and Organizational Effectiveness." In *Handbook of Principles of Organizational Behavior*, edited by Edwin A. Locke, 179–200. Oxford: Blackwell, 2009.

———. "Social Cognitive Theory: An Agentic Perspective." *Annual Review of Psychology* 52 (2001) 1–26.

Bandura, Albert, et al. "Multifaceted Impact of Self-Efficacy Beliefs on Academic Functioning." *Child Development* 67 (1996) 1206–22.

Banks, Cheryl A., and James A. Banks. "Equity Pedagogy: An Essential Component of Multicultural Education." *Theory into Practice* 34:3 (1995) 152–58.

Banks, James A. *Educating Citizens in a Multicultural Society*. 2nd ed. New York: Teachers College Press, 2007.

———. *An Introduction to Multicultural Education*. 2nd ed. Boston: Allyn and Bacon, 1999.

———. "Multicultural Education: Characteristics and Goals." In *Multicultural Education: Issues and Perspectives*, edited by James Banks and Cheryl M. Banks, 3–23. 8th ed. Hoboken, NJ: Wiley, 2013.

Bibliography

Banks, James A., and Cheryl McGee Banks. *Multicultural Education: Issues and Perspectives*. San Francisco: Jossey-Bass, 2005.

Bannister, Nicole A. "Breaking the Spell of Differentiated Instruction through Equity Pedagogy and Teacher Community." *Cultural Studies of Science Education* 11:2 (June 2016) 335–47. https://doi.org/10.1007/s11422–016–9766–0.

Bashant, Jennifer. "Developing Grit in Our Students: Why Grit Is Such a Desirable Trait." *Journal for Leadership and Instruction* 13:2 (Fall 2014) 14–17.

Becktold, Tony H. "Brain Based Instruction in Correctional Settings: Strategies for Teachers." *Journal of Correctional Education* 52:3 (September 2001) 95–97.

Beechick, Ruth. *A Biblical Psychology of Learning: How Your Mind Works*. Denver: Accent, 1982.

Beltman, Susan, et al. "Thriving Not Just Surviving: A Review of Research on Teacher Resilience." *Educational Research Review* 6:3 (January 2011) 185–207. https://doi.org/10.1016/j.edurev.2011.09.001.

Benard, Bonnie. *Resiliency: What We Have Learned*. San Francisco: WestEd, 2004.

Benson, Peter L. "On a Path Toward Thriving." *Reclaiming Children and Youth* 21:1 (Spring 2012) 16–17.

Benson, Peter L., et al. "Spiritual Development in Childhood and Adolescence: Toward Field of Inquiry." *Applied Developmental Science* 7 (2003) 205–13.

Berry, Theodorea R., and Matthew R. Candis. "Cultural Identity and Education: A Critical Race Perspective." *Educational Foundations* 27,:2 (Summer–Fall 2013) 43–64.

Biswas-Diener, et al. "A Dynamic Approach to Psychological Strength Development and Intervention." *The Journal of Positive Psychology* 6:2 (2011) 106–18. https://doi.org/10.1080/17439760.2010.545429.

Blad, Evie. "Measuring the Social and Emotional Sides of Student Success." *Education Week* 36:37 (2017) 4–5.

Bonchek, Mark. "Why the Problem with Learning Is Unlearning." *Harvard Business Review*, Managing Yourself, November 3, 2016. https://hbr.org/2016/11/why-the-problem-with-learning-is-unlearning.

Bondy, Elizabeth, and Dorene D. Ross. "The Teacher as Warm Demander." *Educational Leadership* 66:1 (September 2008) 54–58.

Borich, Gary D. *Effective Teaching Methods: Research-Based Practice*. Boston: Pearson, 2017.

Bourdieu, Pierre. "Systems of Education and Systems of Thought." In *Knowledge and Control: New Directions for the Sociology of Education*, edited by Michael F. D. Young, 189–207. London: Collier-Macmillan, 1971.

Bowles, Samuel, and Herbert Gintis. *Schooling in Capitalist America*. New York: Basic Books, 1976.

Bowman, Richard F. "A New Story about Teaching and Learning." *The Clearing House* 92:3 (2019) 112–17. https://doi.org/10.1080/00098655.2019.1613339.

Boynton, Mark, and Christine Boynton. *Educator's Guide to Preventing and Solving Disciple Problems*. Alexandria, VA: ASCD, 2005.

Brant, Jo-Ann. *John*. Paideia Commentaries on the New Testament. Grand Rapids: Baker, 2011.

Bransford, John D., and Suzanne M. Donovan. *How Students Learn: Science in the Classroom*. Washington, DC: National Academies, 2005.

Brenneman, Ross. "How Teachers Can Build Social-Emotional Learning Skills." *Education Week* 39:2 (August 2019) 14. http://www.edweek.org/media/150305presentation(4pm).pdf.

Briner, Bob, and Ray Pritchard. *The Leadership Lessons of Jesus: A Timeless Model for Today's Leaders.* Nashville: Broadman & Holman, 1997.

Brown, Robert M. *Unexpected News: Reading the Bible with Third World Eyes.* Louisville: Westminster, 1984.

Brunzell, Tom, et al. "Shifting Teacher Practice in Trauma-Affected Classrooms: Practice Pedagogy Strategies within a Trauma-Informed Education Model." *School Mental Health* 11 (2019) 600–614. https://doi.org/10.1007/s12310-018-09308-8.

Buchanan, Mark. "The Benefit of the Doubt: The Disciple Thomas Reveals an Important Truth about Faith." *Christianity Today* 44:4 (April 2000) 62–67.

Burbules, Nicholas. "Jesus as a Teacher." In *Spirituality and Ethics in Education: Philosophical, Theological, and Radical Perspectives*, edited by Alexander Hanan, 7–20. Brighton: Sussex Academic, 2004.

Burwell, Rebecca, and Mackenzie Huyser. "Practicing Hospitality in the Classroom." *Journal of Education and Christian Belief* 17:1 (2013) 9–24.

Cameron, Kim S., and Robert E. Quinn. "Organizational Paradox and Transformation." In *Paradox and Transformation: Toward a Theory of Change in Organization and Management*, edited by Robert E. Quinn and Kim S. Cameron, 1–18. Cambridge: Ballinger, 1988.

Carjuzaa, Ioanna, and Richard Kellough. *Teaching in the Middle and Secondary Schools.* Upper Saddle River, NJ: Pearson, 2016.

Carello, Janice, and Lisa. L. D. Butler. "Practicing What We Teach: Trauma-Informed Educational Practice." *Journal of Teaching in Social Work* 35 (2015) 262–78. https://doi.org/10.1080/08841233.2015.1030059.

Carson, Barbara H. "Thirty Years of Stories: The Professor's Place in Student Memories." *Change* 28 (1996) 10–17.

Cartledge, Gwendolyn, and Joanne F. Milburn. *Teaching Social Skills to Children and Youth: Innovative Approaches.* Boston: Allyn and Bacon. 1995.

Carver, Carver S. "Resilience and Thriving: Issues, Models and Linkage." *Journal of Social Issues* 54 (1998) 245–66.

CASEL (Collaborative for Academic, Social, and Emotional Learning). *Framework for Systemic Social and Emotional Learning.* 2019. https://casel.org/.

————. *Implementing Systemic District and School Social and Emotional Learning.* Chicago: CASEL, 2013.

CDC (Centers for Disease Control and Prevention). *Fourth National Report on Human Exposure to Environmental Chemicals, Updated Tables.* March 2021. Atlanta: U.S. Department of Health and Human Services, 2021.

Chandler, Michael. *The Othello Effect: Essay on the Emergence and Eclipse of Skeptical Doubt, Human Nature and Conduct.* New York: Holt, 1987.

Chickering, Arthur, and Zelda Gamson. "Seven Principles for Good Practice in Undergraduate Education." *AAHE Bulletin* 39:7 (1987) 3–7.

Christenbury, Leila. "The Flexible Teacher." *Educational Leadership* 68:4 (December 2010) 46–50.

Cless, Jessica D., and Brian S. Nelson-Goff. "Teaching Trauma: A Model for Introducing Traumatic Materials in the Classroom." *Advances in Social Work* 18:1 (Spring 2017) 25–38. https://doi.org/10.18060/21177.

Clifton, Donald O., et al. *StrengthsQuest: Discover and Develop Your Strengths in Academics and Career*. New York: Gallup, 2006.

Cohen, Elizabeth G., et al. "Can Expectations for Competence Be Treated in the Classroom?" In *Status Generalization: New Theory and Research*, edited by Murray Webster and Martha Foschi, 27–54. Stanford, CA: Stanford University Press, 1988.

———. "Complex Instruction: Equity in Cooperative Learning Classrooms." *Theory into Practice* 38:2 (Spring 1999) 80–86.

Collins, James. "Social Reproduction in Classrooms and Schools." *Annual Review of Anthropology* 38 (2009) 33–48. https://doi.org/10.1146/annurev.anthro.37.081407.085242.

Conn, Anne-Marie, et al. "Creating a Culture of Care: A School-Based Behavioral Therapy Intervention Builds Resilience for Students with High Levels of Trauma." *Educational Leadership* 78:2 (October 2020) 58–63.

Crosby, Shantel D., et al. "Social Justice Education through Trauma-Informed Teaching." *Middle School Journal* 49:4 (2018) 15–23. https://doi.org/10.1080/00940771.208.14 88470.

Csikszentmihalyi, Mihaly. "Flow: The Psychology of Optimal Experience." *Journal of Leisure Research* 24:1 (1990) 93–94.

Curwin, Richard L., et al. *Discipline with Dignity: How to Build Responsibility, Relationships, and Respect in Your Classroom*. 4th ed. Alexandria, VA: ASCD, 2018.

Darling-Hammond, Linda. "Educating the New Educator: Teacher Education and the Future of Democracy." *New Educator* 1:1 (2005) 1–18.

Delgado, Richard. "Storytelling for Oppositionists and Others: A Plea for Narrative." *Michigan Law Review* 87 (1989) 2411–41.

Devine, Patricia G., and Monteith, Margo J. "The Role of Discrepancy-Associated Affect in Prejudice Reduction." In *Affect, Cognition, and Stereotyping: Interactive Processes in Group Perception*, edited by Diane M. Mackie and David L. Hamilton, 317–44. Cambridge: Academic, 1993.

Diaz, Rico, et al. *The Cross-Cultural Language and Academic Development*. 3rd ed. Boston: Allyn and Bacon, 1996.

Dillard, Cynthia B. "You Are Because I Am: Toward New Covenants of Equity and Diversity in Teacher Education." *Educational Studies* 55:2 (March–April 2019) 121–38. https://doi.org/10.1080/00131946.2018.1523791.

Dinkmeyer, Don, and Rudolf Dreikurs. *Encouraging Children to Learn*. New York: Taylor & Francis, 2000.

DomNwachukwu, Chinaka S. *Introduction to Multicultural Education: From Theory to Practice*. Langham, MD: Rowman & Littlefield, 2010.

DomNwachukwu, Chinaka S., and HeeKap Lee. *Multiculturalism: A Shalom Motif the Christian Community*. Eugene, OR: Wipf & Stock, 2014.

Dover, Alison G. "Teaching for Social Justice: From Conceptual Frameworks to Classroom Practices." *Multicultural Perspectives Education* 15:1 (2013) 3–11. https://doi.org/10.1080/15210960.2013.754285.

———. "Teaching for Social Justice and K–12 Student Outcomes: A Conceptual Framework and Research Review." *Equity & Excellence in Education* 42 (2009) 507–25.

Dovidio, John F., et al. "From Intervention to Outcome: Processes in the Reduction of Bias." In *Education Programs for Improving Intergroup Relations: Theory, Research, and Practice*, edited by Walter G. Stephan and W. Paul Vogt, 243–65. New York: Teachers College, 2004.

Dreikurs, Rudolf. *Psychology in the Classroom: A Manual for Teachers*. New York: Harper & Row, 1968.

Duckworth, Angela. *Grit: The Power of Passion and Perseverance*. New York: Scribner, 2016

Duckworth, Angela L., et al. "Grit: Perseverance and Passion for Long-term Goals." *Journal of Personality and Social Psychology* 92 (2007) 1087–101.

Durlak, Joseph, et al. "The Impact of Enhancing Students' Social and Emotional Learning: A Meta-Analysis of School-Based Universal Interventions." *Child Development* 82 (2011) 405–32.

Dweck, Carol S. "Messages that Motivate: How Praise Molds Students' Beliefs, Motivation, and Performance in Surprising Ways." In *Improving Academic Achievement: Impact of Psychological Factors on Education*, edited by J. Aronson, 37–60. Orlando, FL: Academic, 2002.

———. *Mindset: The New Psychology of Success*. New York: Ballantine, 2016.

———. "Mindsets and Human Nature: Promoting Change in the Middle East, the Schoolyard, the Racial Divide, and Willpower." *American Psychologist* 67:8 (2012) 614–22.

———. "Motivational Processes Affecting Learning." *American Psychologist* 41:10 (1986) 1040–48.

Dweck, Carol S., and Ellen L. Leggett. "A Social-Cognitive Approach to Motivation and Personality." *Psychological Review* 95:2 (1988) 256.

Elias, Marilyn. "The School-to-Prison Pipeline." *Teaching Tolerance* 43 (Spring 2013) 39–40.

Elkins, David N., et al. "Toward a Humanistic-Phonological Spirituality: Definition, Description, and Measurement." *Journal of Humanistic Psychology* 28 (1988) 5–18.

Epitropoulos, Alexa. "10 Signs of a Toxic School Culture." *Education Update* 61:9 (September 2019) 14–15.

Erdman, Sarah., et al. "Preventing Compassion Fatigue: Caring Yourself." *Young Children* 75:3 (July 2020) 28–35.

Erikson, Erik. *Identity: Youth and Crisis*. New York: Norton, 1968.

Fagell, Phyllis. "Coping with Change and Uncertainty." *Educational Leadership* 78:4 (January 2021) 22–26.

Fagin, Gerald M. "A Doubter Gives Lessons in Faith." *America* 197 (2007) 22–23.

Fallot, Roger D. and Harris, Maxine. "Creating Cultures of Trauma-Informed Care (CCTIC): A Self-Assessment and Planning Protocol." *Community Connections*, 2009. http://www.healthcare.uiowa.edu/ icmh/documents/CCTICSelf-Assessment andPlanningProtocolo709.pdf.

Fantigrossi, Joseph D. "Creating Safe and Supportive Schools: A Community Schools Model at Work." *Journal of Higher Education Theory and Practice* 20:6 (2020) 31–34.

Farrington, Camille A., et al. *The Role of Noncognitive Factors in Shaping School Performance: A Critical Literature Review*. Chicago: University of Chicago Consortium on Chicago School Research, 2012.

Feeney, Brooke C., and Nancy L. Collins. "Thriving through Relationships." *Current Opinion in Psychology* 1 (2015) 22–28.

Forbes, Catherine, and Peter Kaufman. "Critical Pedagogy in the Sociology Classroom: Challenges and Concerns." *Teaching Sociology* 36:1 (January 2008) 26–33.

Freire, Paulo. *Pedagogy of the Oppressed.* New York: Continuum, 1970.

———. *Teachers as Cultural Workers: Letters to Those Who Dare Teach.* Boulder, CO: Westview, 1998.

Gallagher, Eugene V. "Welcoming the Stranger." *Teaching Theology and Religion* 10:3 (2007) 137–42.

Garbarino, James. "Educating Children in a Socially Toxic Environment." *Educational Leadership* 54:7 (April 1997) 12–16.

———. *Raising Children in a Socially Toxic Environment.* San Francisco: Jossey-Bass, 1995.

Gabrieli, C., et al. *Ready to Be Counted: The Research Case for Education Policy Action on Non-Cognitive Skills.* Boston: Transforming Education, 2015.

Garber, David G. "Trauma Theory and Biblical Studies." *Currents in Biblical Research* 14:1 (October 2015) 24–44.

Gardner, Morgan, and Angela Crockwell. "Engaging Democracy and Social Justice in Creating Educational Alternatives: An Account of Voice and Agency for Marginalized Youth and the Community." *Innovation Journal: The Public Sector Innovation Journal* 11:3 (2006) 1–19.

Geraty, Ronald. "Education and Self-Esteem." In *The Development and Sustenance of Self-Esteem in Childhood,* edited by J. E. Mack and S. L. Ablon, 255–69. New York: International Universities, 1983.

Gersch, Irvine. "A Positive Future for Educational Psychology." *Educational Psychology in Practice* 15:1 (March 2009) 9–19.

Gill, David W. "Eight Traits of an Ethically Healthy Culture: Insights from the Beatitudes." *Journal of Markets & Morality* 16:2 (Fall 2013) 615–33.

Giroux, Henry A. "Democracy, Education, and Politics of Critical Pedagogy." In *Critical Pedagogy: Where Are We Now?,* edited by Peter McLaren and Joe L. Kincheole, 81–100. New York: Peter Lang, 2007.

———. "Postmodernism and the Discourse of Educational Criticism." In *Postmodern Education, Politics, Culture and Social Criticism,* 57–86. Minneapolis: University of Minnesota Press, 1991.

———. "Rethinking Education as the Practice of Freedom: Paulo Freire and the Promise of Critical Pedagogy." *Policy Futures in Education* 8:6 (2010) 715–25.

———. *Teachers as Intellectuals: Toward a Critical Pedagogy of Learning.* South Hadley, MA: Bergin & Garvey, 1988.

Glazzard, Jonathan. "Perceptions of the Barriers to Effective Inclusion in One Primary School: Voices of Teachers and Teaching Assistance." *Support for Learning* 26:2 (2011) 56–63

Goddard, Roger D., and Yvonne L. Goddard. "A Multilevel Analysis of the Relationship Between Teacher and Collective Efficacy in Urban Schools." *Teaching and Teacher Education* 17:7 (2001) 807–18.

Goddard, Roger D., et al. "Collective Teacher Efficacy: Its Meaning, Measure, and Effect on Student Achievement." *American Education Research Journal* 37:2 (2000) 479–507.

Golden, John, and Lisa Storm Fink. "A Conversation with Linda Christensen on Social Justice Education." *English Journal* 97:6 (July 2008) 59–64.

Gould, Paul M. *The Outrageous Idea of the Missional Professor.* Eugene, OR: Wipf & Stock, 2014.

Gorski, Paul. *Multicultural Education and the Internet: Intersection and Integrations.* Boston: McGraw-Hill, 2005.

Grant, Carl A., and Christine E. Sleeter. "Race, Class, Gender and Disability in the Classroom." In *Multicultural Education: Issues and Perspectives,* edited by James A. Banks and Cheryl M. Banks, 43–62. 8th ed. Hoboken, NJ: Wiley, 2013.

Greene, Katie. "Collaboration, Texts and Team Building: Creating Opportunities for Conversation and Understanding." *English Journal* 106:1 (September 2016) 13–16.

Greenstein, Laura. *Assessing 21st Century Skills: A Guide to Evaluating Mastery and Authentic Learning.* Thousand Oaks, CA: Corwin, 2012.

Gruenert, Steve, and Todd Whitaker. *School Culture Rewired: How to Define, Assess, and Transform it.* Alexandria, Alexandria, VA: ASCD, 2015.

Gutierrez, Daniel, and Andrea Gutierrez, "Developing a Trauma-Informed Lens in the College Classroom and Empowering Students through Building Positive Relationship." *Contemporary Issues in Education Research* 12:1 (2019) 11–18.

Haggis, Diane. "Influencing Positive Outcomes for Troubled Youth." *Contemporary Issues in Education Research* 10:3 (2017). https://files.eric.ed.gov/fulltext/EJ1147267.pdf.

———. *Teacher Perceptions of What They Do in Their Institutionalized Settings to Create a Positive Learning Environment for Troubled Youth in Their Classrooms.* Ann Arbor, MI: ProQuest, 2011.

Hahn, Roger L. *Matthew: A Commentary for Bible Students.* Indianapolis: Wesleyan House, 2007.

Halbhavi, S., et al. "The Leadership Imperative." *Technology & Learning* 26:4 (2005) 12–13.

Hammond, Zaretta. *Culturally Responsive Teaching and the Brain: Promoting Authentic Engagement and Rigor among Culturally and Linguistically Diverse Students.* Thousand Oaks, CA: Corwin, 2015.

Hanish, Laura, et al. "Social Harmony in Schools." In *Handbook on Social-Emotional, Motivation, and Cognitive Outcomes in School Context,* edited by Kathryn Wentzel and Geetha Ramani, 48–59. Oxfordshire: Taylor & Francis, 2016.

Hansman Catherine A. "Context-Based Adult Learning." *New Directions for Adult and Continuing Education* 89 (Spring 2005) 43–51.

Hansen, Edmund J. "Creating Teachable Moments and Making Them Last." *Innovative Higher Education* 23:1 (Fall 1998) 7–26.

Hanson, Janet L. *Manage Your Mindset: Maximize Your Power of Personal Choice.* Lanham, MD: Rowman & Littlefield, 2017.

Hardiman, R., et al. "Conceptual Foundations for Social Justice Education." In *Teaching for Diversity and Social Justice,* edited by M. Adams et al., 35–66. 2nd ed. New York: Routledge.

Harry, E. "Minority Disproportionality in Special Education." In *Encyclopedia of the Social and Cultural Foundations of Education,* edited by Eugene F. Provenzo and Asterie Baker Provenzo, 502–4. Los Angeles: SAGE, 2008. http://www.sage-ereference.com.

Hart, Caroline S. "Education, Inequality and Social Justice: A Critical Analysis Applying the Sen-Bourdieu Analytical Framework." *Policy Futures in Education* 17:5 (2018) 582–98. https://doi.org/10.1177/1478210318809758.

Haymovitz, Ethan, et al. "Exploring the Perceived Benefits and Limitations of a School-Based Social-Emotional Learning Program: A Concept Map Evaluation." *Children & Schools* 40:1 (January 2018) 45–54. https://doi.org/10.1093/cs/cdx029.

Hendrickson, Jo, et al. "UI REACH: A Postsecondary Program Serving Students with Autism and Intellectual Disabilities." *Education and Treatment of Children* 36:4 (2013) 169–94.

Bibliography

Herzberg, Frederick, Bernard Mausner, and Barbara Snyderman. *The Motivation to Work.* New York: Wiley, 1959.

Hester, Michael. "A Theology for Family Ministry." *Review and Expositor* 86:2 (1989) 161–73.

Hoare, Carol. "The Toxic Effect on Children of a Degraded U.S. Society, Family, and Educational Context: How Will This Nation Respond?" *Integral Review* 4:2 (December 2008) 106–17.

Hoerr, Thomas R. *The Formative Five: Fostering Grit, Empathy, and Other Success Skills Every Student Needs.* Alexandria, VA: ASCD, 2016.

Honsinger, Connie, and Marvis Hendricks Brown. "Preparing Trauma-Sensitive Teachers: Strategies for Teacher Educators." *Teacher Education Journal* 12 (Spring 2019) 129–52.

Hoy, Wayne K., and Scott R. Sweetland. "Designing Better Schools: The Meaning and Nature of Enabling School Structure." *Educational Administration Quarterly* 37:3(2001) 296–321.

Hoy, Wayne K., et al. "Academic Optimism of Schools: A Force for Student Achievement." *American Educational Research Journal* 43 (2006) 425–46.

Hoyer, Stephen, and Patrice McDaniel. "From Jericho to Jerusalem: The Good Samaritan from a Different Direction." *Journal of Psychology and Theology* 18:4 (1990) 326–33.

Hughes, Daniel A. *Attachment-Focused Parenting: Effective Strategies to Care for Children.* New York: Norton, 2009.

Hyland, Nora E. "Social Justice in Early Childhood Classrooms What the Research Tells Us." *Young Children* 65:1 (January 2010) 82–90.

Hytten, Kathy, and Silvia C. Bettez. "Understanding Education for Social Justice." *Educational Foundations* 25:1 (Spring 2011) 7–24.

James, Glenn, et al. "What Can Jesus Teach Us about Student Engagement." *Journal of Catholic Education* 19:1 (September 2015) 129–54. https://doi.org/10.15365/joice.1901062015.

Jankiewicz, Darius, and Edyta Jankiewicz. "Let the Little Children Come." *Andrew University Seminary Studies* 49:2 (2011) 213–42.

Jennings, Patricia A. "Teaching in a Trauma-Sensitive Classroom." *American Educator* 43:2 (Summer 2019) 12–17. https://www.aft.org/ae/summer2019/jennings.

Jensen, Eric. *Brain-Based Learning.* 2nd ed. Thousand Oaks, CA: Corwin, 2008.

———. *Teaching with Poverty in Mind.* Alexandria, VA: ASCD, 2009.

Jonas, Robert A. *Henri Nouwen.* Maryknoll, NY: Orbis, 1998.

Kagan, Spencer. "Teaching for Character and Community." *Educational Leadership* 59:2 (October 2001) 50–55.

Kay, Lisa, and Denise Wolf. "Artful Coalitions: Challenging Adverse Adolescent Experiences." *Art Education* 70:5 (2017) 26–33.

Keown, Stacey, et al. "Creating a Community of Caring within a School." *International Electronic Journal of Elementary Education* 12:4 (March 2020) 401–4. https://doi.org/10.26822/iejee.2020459469.

Kirkpatrick, Donald L., and James D.Kirkpatrick. *Evaluating Training Programs.* San Francisco: Berrett-Koehler, 1996.

Kitwood, Tom. *Dementia Reconsidered: The Person Comes First.* Buckingham: Open University Press, 1997.

Knight, Eric, and Sotirios Paroutis. "Expanding the Paradox-Pedagogy Links: Paradox as a Threshold Concept in Management Education." In *The Oxford Handbook of*

Organizational Paradox, edited by Wendy K. Smith et al. Oxford: Oxford University Press, 2017. https://doi.org/10.1093/oxfordhb/9780198754428.013.31.

Knight, George. *Philosophy and Education: An Introduction in Christian Perspective.* Berrien Springs, MI: Andrews University Press, 2006.

Kohm, Barbara, and Beverly Nance. "Creating Collaborative Cultures." *Educational Leadership* 67:2 (October 2009) 67–72.

Kristjansson, Kristjan. "Positive Psychology and Positive Education." *Educational Psychologist* 47:2 (2012) 86–105.

Lamperes, Bill. "Empowering At-Risk Students to Succeed." *Educational Leadership* 52:3 (November 1994) 67–70.

Langer, Ellen J. *The Power of Mindful Learning.* New York: Addison-Wesley, 1997.

Langer, Richard, et al. "Human Flourishing: The Context for Character Development in Christian Higher Education." *Christian Higher Education* 9 (2010) 336–60.

Laursen, Erik K. "The Power of Grit, Perseverance and Tenacity." *Reclaiming Children and Youth* 23:4 (Winter 2015) 19–24.

Leadbeater, Charles. "It's All About Relationships." *Educational Leadership* 66:3 (November 2008). http://www.ascd.org/publications/educational-leadership/nov08/vol66/num03/It's-All-About-Relationships.aspx.

Leaf, Caroline. *Switch on Your Brain: The Key to Peak Happiness, Thinking, and Health.* Grand Rapids: Baker, 2013.

———. *Think, Learn, Succeed: Understanding and Using Your Mind to Thrive at School, the Workplace, and Life.* Grand Rapids: Baker, 2018.

Ledesma, Janet. "Conceptual Frameworks and Research Models on Resilience in Leadership." *SAGE Open* 4:3 (July 2014) 1–8. https://doi.org/10.1177/2158244014545464.

Lee, HeeKap. "'Jesus Teaching' through Discovery." *International Christian Community of Teacher Educators Journal* 1:2 (2006). https://digitalcommons.georgefox.edu/icctej/vol1/iss2/5/.

Lee, HeeKap, and IeMay Freeman. "Three Models of Constructivist Learning Utilized by Jesus." In *Integrating Faith and Special Education: A Christian Faith Approach to Special Education Practice*, edited by Ben Nworie, 153–67. Eugene, OR: Wipf & Stock, 2016.

Lee, HeeKap, and Ruth Givens. "Critical Consciousness and the Christian Consciousness: Making the Necessary Connections between Faith-Based Learning and Critical Pedagogy." *Journal of Research on Christian Education* 21:3 (2012) 195–210.

Lenox, Mary F. "Storytelling for Young Children in a Multicultural World." *Early Childhood Education Journal* 28:2 (2000) 97–103.

Lewin, Kurt. "Group Decisions and Social Change." In *Readings in Social Psychology*, edited by Eleanor E. Maccobby et al., 330–44, New York: Holt, Rinehart & Winston, 1958.

Lewis, C. S. *The Lion, the Witch, and the Wardrobe.* New York: Harper Trophy, 1978.

Lewis, Karoline. M. "Shepherd My Sheep: Preaching for the Sake of Greater Works than These." *Word & World* 28:3 (Summer 2008) 318–24.

Lewis, Mrianne W., and Gordon E. Dehler. "Learning through Paradox: A Pedagogical Strategy for Exploring Contradictions and Complexity." *Journal of Management Education* 24:6 (December 2000) 708–25.

Lickona, Thomas. *Educating for Character: How Our Schools Can Teach Respect and Responsibility.* New York: Bantam, 1991.

————. "The Return of Character Education." *Educational Leadership* 51:3 (November 1993) 6–11.

Lioy, Dan. "A Comparative Analysis of Psalm 1 and the Beatitudes in Matthew 5:3–12." *Conspectus* 22 (October 2016) 141–82.

Lipman, Matthew. "Critical Thinking: What Can It Be?" *Educational Leadership* 46:1 (September 1988) 38–43.

Lopez, Shane J., and Michelle C. Louis. "The Principles of Strength-Based Education." *Journal of College & Character* 10:4 (April 2009) 1–8. https://doi.org/10.2202/1940-1639.1041.

Losinski, Micky, et al. "Schools as Change Agents in Reducing Bias and Discrimination: Shaping Behaviors and Attitudes." *Journal of Child and Family Studies* 28:10 (October 2019) 2718–26.

Luthans, Fred, et al. *Psychological Capital: Developing the Human Competitive Edge.* Oxford: Oxford University, 2007.

Mackenzie, Susan Hough, et al. "Unifying Psychology and Experiential Education." *Journal of Experiential Education* 37:1 (2014) 75–88.

Marmon, Ellen L. "Teaching as Hospitality." *Asbury Theological Journal* 63:2 (2008) 33–39.

Martin, Ryan. "The Five Finger Challenge: Knowing Students More Deeply." *Teachers Matter* 47 (2020) 20.

Marx, Gary. *Sixteen Trends, Their Profound Impact on Our Future: Implications for Students, Education, Communities, and the Whole of Society.* Alexandria, VA: Educational Research Service, 2006.

Maslow, Abraham H. *Motivation and Personality.* New York: Harper, 1954.

————. *The Psychology of Science: A Renaissance.* Chicago: Regnery, 1970.

————. "A Theory of Human Motivation." *Psychological Review* 50:4 (1943) 370–96.

Massari, Lauri. "Teaching Emotional Intelligence." *Leadership* 40:5 (May 2011) 8–12.

Mayer, G. Roy. "Behavioral Strategies to Reduce School Violence." *Child & Family Behavior Therapy* 24:1–2 (2002) 83–100.

McAfee, Robert B. *Unexpected News: Reading the Bible with Third World Eyes.* Louisville: Westminster John Knox, 1984.

McClure, Jennifer M. "Introducing Jesus' Social Network: Support, Conflict and Compassion." *Interdisciplinary Journal of Research on Religion* 12 (2016) 1–22.

McElhaney, Kathleen B., et al. "They Like Me, They Like Me Not: Popularity and Adolescents' Perceptions of Acceptance." *Child Development* 79 (2008) 493–513.

McEwan, Rhonda M., et al. "Cultivating Hope through Learning for the Common Good." *Christian Higher Education* 15:5 (2016) 307–19. https://doi.org/10.1080/15363759.2016.1211038.

McGee, John, et al. *Gentle Teaching: A Nonaversive Approach for Helping Persons with Mental Retardation.* New York: Human Sciences, 1987.

McGee, John, and Marge Brown. *Gentle Teaching Primer.* Creative Options Regina, 2014. https://creativeoptionsregina.ca/wp-content/uploads/2015/03/Gentle-Teaching-Primer-2014.pdf.

McHugh, Adam S. *The Listening Life: Embracing Attentiveness in a World of Distraction.* Downers Grove, IL: InterVarsity, 2015.

McIntyre, James R. "Assessing Student Performance and School Success with Non-Cognitive Measures." Presented at the Annual AASA convention, Los Angeles, CA, February 2013.

McLaren, Peter. *Life in Schools: An Introduction to Critical Pedagogy in the Foundations of Education.* 6th ed. New York: Longman, 2015.

McMillan, James. *Classroom Assessment: Principles and Practice for Effective Standards-Based Instruction.* 6th ed. Boston: Allyn & Bacon, 2014.

Medina, John. *Brain Rules: 12 Principles for Surviving and Thriving at Work, Home, and School.* Seattle: Pear, 2014.

Mehta, Jai. *How Social and Emotional Learning Can Succeed.* American Enterprise Institute, May 2020. https://files.eric.ed.gov/fulltext/ED606307.pdf.

Melnick, Hanna, and Lorea Martinez. *Preparing Teachers to Support Social and Emotional Learning: A Case Study of San Jose State University and Lakewood Elementary School.* Palo Alto, CA: Learning Policy Institute, 2019.

Mergler, Mary Schmid, et al. "Alternative Discipline Can Benefit Learning." *Phi Delta Kappan* 96:2 (October 2014) 25–30.

Michon, Cyrille. "Believing God: An Account of Faith as Personal Trust." *Religious Studies* 53 (2017) 387–401. https://doi.org/10.1017/S0034412517000270.

Miller, Alistair. "A Critique of Positive Psychology or the New Science of Happiness." *Journal of Philosophy of Education* 42:3–4 (2008) 591–608.

Minahan, Jessica. "Trauma-Informed Teaching Strategies." *Educational Leadership* 77:2 (October 2019) 30–36.

Mole, Phil. "Skepticism in the Classroom: A High School Science Teacher in the Trends." *Skeptic* 12:3 (2006) 62–70.

Moneyhun, Clyde. "Believing, Doubting, Deciding, Acting." *Journal for the Assembly for Expanded Perspectives on Learning (JAEPL)* 15 (Winter 2009) 54–62.

Motyer, Alec. *The Message of Philippians.* Downers Grove, IL: InterVarsity, 1984.

Newhouse, Kara. "Four Core Priorities for Trauma-Informed Distance Learning." KQED, MindShift, April 6, 2020. https://www.kqed.org/mindshift/55679/four-core-priorities-for-trauma-informed-distance-learning.

Nieto, Sonia. "Identity, Personhood, and Puerto Rican Students: Challenging Paradigms of Assimilation and Authenticity." *Journal for the Scholar-Practitioner Quarterly* 1:4 (2004) 41–62.

Nieto, Sonia, and Patty Body. *School Reform and Student Learning: A Multicultural Perspective.* Hoboken, NJ: Wiley, 2010.

Nodding, Nel. *Caring: A Feminine Approach to Ethics and Moral Education.* Los Angeles: University of California Press, 2013.

———. *Happiness and Education.* New York: Cambridge, 2003.

Nord, Warren. *Religion and American Education: Rethinking a National Dilemma.* Chapel Hill: University of North Carolina Press, 1995.

Nouwen, Henri J. M. *Creative Ministry.* New York: Image, 1971.

———. *Reaching Out: The Three Movements of the Spiritual Life.* New York: Image, 1975.

———. *Spiritual Direction: Wisdom for the Long Walk of Faith.* York: Harper One, 2006.

———. *The Wounded Healer: Ministry in Contemporary Society.* New York: Image, 1979.

Nugent Nicole R., et al. "Resilience after Trauma: From Surviving to Thriving." *European Journal of Psychotraumatology* 5 (2014). https://doi.org/10.3402/ejpt.v5.25339.

O'Collins, Gerald. "An Easter Healing of Memories." *America* 166:13 (April 1992) 322–23.

O'Leary, Virginia E. "Strength in the Face of Adversity: Individual and Social Thriving." *Journal of Social Issues* 54 (1998) 425–46.

O'Leary, Virginia E., and Jeanette R. Ickovics. "Resilience and Thriving in Response to Challenge: An Opportunity for a Paradigm Shift in Women's Health." *Women's Health: Resilience on Gender, Behavior, and Policy* 1 (1995) 121–42.

Olson, Steve. *From Neuron to Neighborhood: An Update.* Washington, DC: National Academic, 2012.

Osterman, Karen F. "Students' Need for Belonging in the School Community." *Review of Educational Research* 70:3 (2000) 323–67. https://doi.org/10.3102/00346543070003323.

Otieno, Tabatha. N. "The Learning and Inquiry." *Canadian Journal for the Scholarship of Teaching and Learning* 3:1 (2012) 1–20.

Palmer, Parker. *The Courage to Teach: Exploring the Inner Landscape of a Teacher's Life.* 10th ed. San Francisco: Jossey-Bass, 2017.

————. *The Promise of Paradox: A Celebration of Contradictions in the Christian Life.* San Francisco: Jossey-Bass, 1993.

————. *To Know as We are Known: Education as a Spiritual Journey.* San Francisco: Harper, 1993.

Pang, Valerie Ooka. *Multicultural Education: A Caring-Centered, Reflective Approach.* Boston: McGraw-Hill, 2001.

Pappano Laura. "Grit and the New Character Education." *Education Digest* 78:9 (May 2013) 4–19.

Parchomiuk, Monika. "Teacher Empathy and Attitudes towards Individuals with Disabilities." *International Journal of Disabilities, Development and Education* 66:1 (2019) 56–69.

Park, Nansook. "Building Strengths of Character: Keys to Positive Youth Development." *Reclaiming Children and Youth* 18:2 (Summer 2009) 42–47.

Parker, Jessica, and Jenny Folkman. "Building Resilience in Students at the Intersection of Special Education and Foster Care: Challenges, Strategies, and Resources for Educators." *Issues in Teacher Education* 24:2 (Fall 2015) 43–62.

Pate, Alexs. *The Innocent Classroom: Dismantling Racial Bias to Support Students of Color.* Alexandra, VA: ASCD, 2020.

Pazos-Rego, Ana. "Learning Disabilities and English Language Learners." In *Encyclopedia of the Social and Cultural Foundations of Education,* edited by Eugene F. Provenzo and Asterie Baker Provenzo. Los Angeles: SAGE, 2008. http://www.sage-ereference.com.

Pearsall, Paul. *The Beethoven Factor: The Positive Psychology of Hardiness, Happiness, Healing and Hope.* Charlottesville, VA: Hampton Roads, 2003.

Perry, Yvonne. "Achievement Gap." In *Encyclopedia of the Social and Cultural Foundations of Education,* edited by Eugene F. Provenzo and Asterie Baker Provenzo. Los Angeles: SAGE, 2008. http://www.sage-ereference.com.

Persell, Caroline. *Social Class and Educational Equality.* Hoboken, NJ: Wiley, 2010.

Picower, Bree. "Using Their Words: Six Elements of Social Justice Curriculum Design for Elementary Classroom." *International Journal of Multicultural Education* 14:1 (2012) 1–17.

Pepler, Debra. "Bullying Interventions: A Binocular Perspective." *Journal of Canadian Academic Child Adolescent Psychiatry* 15:1 (2006) 16–20.

Perkins-Gough, Deborah. "The Significance of Grit: A Conversation with Angela Lee Duckworth." *Educational Leadership* 71:1 (September 2013) 14–20.

Perry, William. *Forms of Intellectual and Ethical Development in the College Years: A Scheme*. New York: Holt, Rinehart & Winston, 1970.

Peterson, Kent D., and Terrence E. Deal. "How Leaders Influence the Culture of Schools." *Educational Leadership* 56:1 (September 1998) 28–30.

———. *Shaping School Culture: Pitfalls, Paradoxes, and Promises*. 2nd ed. San Francisco: Jossey-Bass, 2009.

Pettigrew, Thomas F. "Intergroup Contact: Theory, Research, and New Perspectives." In *Handbook of Research on Multicultural Education*, edited by James A. Banks and Cheryl M. Banks, 770–81. 2nd ed. San Francisco: Jossey-Bass, 2004.

Philip, Esler. "Jesus and the Reduction of Intergroup Conflict: The Parable of the Good Samaritan in the Light of Social Identity Theory." *Biblical Interpretation* 8:4 (October 2000) 325–57. https://doi.org/10.1163/156851500750118953.

Piaget, Jean. *The Equilibrium of Cognitive Structures: The Central Problem of Intellectual Development*. Chicago: University of Chicago Press, 1985.

Pica-Smith, Cinzia, and Christian Scannell. "Teaching and Learning for This Moment: How a Trauma-Informed Lens Can Guide Our Praxis." *International Journal of Multidisciplinary Perspectives in Higher Education* 5:1 (2020) 76–83.

Picower, Bree. "Using Their Words: Six Elements of Social Justice Curriculum Design for the Elementary Classroom." *International Journal of Multicultural Education* 14:1 (2012) 1–17.

Ponds, Kenneth T. "Spiritual Development with Youth." *Reclaiming Children and Youth* 23:1 (Spring 2014) 58–61.

Ponton, Michael, and Nancy Rhea. "Autonomous Learning from a Social Cognitive Perspective." *New Horizons in Adult Education and Human Resource Development* 20:2 (2006) 38–49.

Rawana, Justin R., et al. "The Application of a Strength-Based Approach of Students Behaviors to the Development of a Character Education: Curriculum for Elementary and Secondary Schools." *The Journal of Educational Thought* 45:2 (Autumn 2011) 127–44.

Reich, Robert B. *Education and the Next Economy*. Washington, DC: National Education Association, 1988.

Richards, Lawrence O., and Gary J. Bredfeldt. *Creative Bible Teaching*. Chicago: Moody, 1988.

Robertson, Douglas R. "Generative Paradox in Learner-Centered College Teaching." *Innovative Higher Education* 29:3 (Spring 2005) 181–94. https://doi.org/10.1007/s10755-005-1935-0.

———. "Integrity in Learner-Centered Teaching. In *To Improve the Academy*, edited by Catherine M. Wehlburg and Sandra Chadwick-Blossey, 196–211, Boston: Anker, 2003.

Robinson-Zabartu, Carol, et al. *Teaching 21 Thinking Skills for the 21st Century: The MiCOSA Model*. Boston: Pearson, 2015.

Rogers, Carl. *Client-Centered Therapy: Its Current Practice, Implications and Theory*. London: Constable, 1951.

Rosenthal, Robert, and Lenore Jacobson. *Pygmalion in the Classroom: Teacher Expectation and Pupils' Intellectual Development*. New York: Holt, Rinehart & Winston, 1968.

Rothbart, Myron, et al. "Stereotyping and Sampling Biases in Intergroup Perception." In *Attitudinal Judgment*, edited by J. Richard Eiser, 109–34. New York: Springer, 1984.

Rothenberg, A. *The Emerging Goddess: The Creative Process in Art, Science, and Other Fields*. Chicago: University of Chicago Press, 1979.

Ruble-Davies, Christine. *Becoming a High Expectation Teacher: Raising the Bar*. New York: Routledge, 2008.

Ruiz, Elsa Cantú, and Norma E. Cantú. "Teaching the Teachers: Dismantling Racism and Teaching for Social Change." *Urban Review* 45 (2013) 74–88. https://doi.org/10.1007/s11256-012-0225-2.

Ryan, Richard M., and Edward L. Deci. "Intrinsic and Extrinsic Motivations: Classic Definitions and New Directions." *Contemporary Educational Psychology* 25:1 (2000) 54–67.

Safir, Shane. "Becoming a Warm Demander." *Educational Leadership* 76:6 (March 2019) 64–69.

Salend, Spencer J. *Creating Inclusive Classrooms: Effective and Reflective Practices*. Upper Saddle River, NJ: Pearson, 201.

SAMHSA (Substance Abuse and Mental Health Services Administration). *Results from the 2012 National Survey on Drug Use and Health: Mental Health Findings*. NSDUH Series H-47. HHS Publication (SMA) 13–4805. Rockville, MD: SAMSA, 2013. https://www.samhsa.gov/data/sites/default/files/NSDUHmhfr2012/NSDUHmhfr2012.pdf.

———. *SAMHSA's Concept of Trauma and Guidance for a Trauma-Informed Approach*. Rockville, MD: SAMSA, 2014. ncsacw.samhsa.gov/userfiles/files/SAMHSA_Trauma.pdf.

Saphier, Jon. "The Equitable Classroom: Today's Diverse Student Body Needs Culturally Proficient Teachers." *The Learning Professional* 38:6 (December 2017) 28–31.

Sapon-Shevin, Mara. "Teachable Moments for Social Justice." *Independent School* 67:3 (Spring 2009) 44–47.

Schechter, Chen. "Doubt, Doubting and the Principal's Role: Exploring an Emerging Perspective for School Change." *International Journal of Educational Reform* 15:1 (2006) 2–12.

Schechter, Chen, and Sherry Ganon-Shilon. "Reforming Schools: The Collective Doubting Perspective." *International Journal of Educational Management* 29:1 (2015) 62–72.

Scheffler, Eben. "Empathy for the Psychological Underdog: A Positive Psychological Approach to Luke's Gospel." *Hervormde Theologies Studies* 70:1 (2014) 1–8.

Schnitker, Sarah A., and Robert A. Emmons. "Hegel's Thesis-Antithesis-Synthesis Model." In *Encyclopedia of Sciences and Religions*, edited by A. Runehov and L. Oviedo L., 488–92. Dordrecht, Netherlands: Springer, 1994. https://doi.org/10.1007/978-1-4020-8265-8_200183.

Schoonmaker, Frances. "Only Those Who See Take Off Their Shoes: Seeing the Classroom as a Spiritual Space." *Teachers College Record* 111 (2009) 12.

Schreiner, Laurie A. "Thriving in the Second Year of College: Pathways to Success." *New Directions for Higher Education* 183:9 (2018) 9–21. https://doi.org/10.1002/he.20289.

Seamands, David. *Healing for Damaged Emotions*. Wheaton, IL: Victor, 1992.

———. *Healing of Memories*. Wheaton, IL: Victor, 1989.

Seligman, Martin E. P. "Learned Helplessness." *Annual Review of Medicine* 23:1 (1972) 407–12. https://doi.org/10.1146/annurev.me.23.020172.002203.

Seligman, Martin E. P., et al. "Positive Education: Positive Psychology and Classroom Interventions." *Oxford Review of Education* 35:3 (June 2009) 293–311.

Seligman, Martin E. P., et al. "Positive Psychotherapy." *American Psychologist* 61:8 (2006) 774–88. https://doi.org/10.1037/0003-066X.61.8.774.

Sewell, Alison. "Evoking Children's Spirituality in the Reciprocal Relationships of a Learning Community." *International Journal of Children's Spirituality* 14:1 (February 2009) 5–16.

Shanmugavelu, Ganesan. "Inquiry Method in the Teaching and Learning Process." *International Journal of Education* 8:3 (June 2020) 6–9.

Sheasley Chelsey. "Building a School Like a Tight-Knit Family." Edutopia, 2019. https://www.edutopia.org/article/building-school-tight-knit-family.

Shephard, David. "Do You Love Me?" *Journal of Biblical Literature* 129:4 (2010) 777–92.

Short, Paula M., et al. "Creating Empowered Schools: Lessons in Change." *Journal of Educational Research* 32:4 (1994) 38–52.

Siegel, Harvey. *Educating Reason.* New York: Routledge, 1988.

Simeon, Diana. "Got Grit? Why It Matters." *Your Teen* 42 (Winter 2013) 22–26.

Smith, Moody D. *John: Abingdon New Testament Commentaries.* Nashville: Abingdon, 1999.

Solomon, Charles R. *The Rejection Syndrome: The Need for Genuine Love & Acceptance,* Wheaton, IL: Tyndale, 1983.

Souers, Kritin, and Peter Hall. *Fostering Resilient Learners: Strategies for Creating a Trauma-Sensitive Classroom.* Alexandria, VA: ASCD, 2016.

Stamm, Beth Hudnall. "Measuring Compassion Satisfaction as Well as Fatigue: Developmental History of the Compassion Satisfaction and Fatigue Test." In *Treating Compassion Fatigue,* edited by Charles R. Figley, 107–19. London: Taylor & Francis, 2002.

Stangor, Charles. "The Study of Stereotyping, Prejudice, and Discrimination within Social Psychology." In *Handbook of Prejudice, Stereotyping and Discrimination,* edited by Todd D. Noelson, 1–22. New York: Psychology, 2009.

Stapleton, Ruth C. *The Gift of Inner Healing.* Waco, TX: Word, 1976.

Steel, Claude M. "A Threat in the Air: How Stereotypes Shape Intellectual Identity and Performance." *American Psychologist* 52:6 (1997) 613–29.

Steiner-Adair, Catherine. "Got Grit: The Call to Educate Smart, Savvy, and Socially Intelligent Students in the Digital Age." *Independent School Magazine* 72:2 (Winter 2013) 28–32.

Strong, Zoe, H. and Emma M. McMain. "Social Justice Learning for Social Emotional Justice: A Conceptual Framework for Education in the Midst of Pandemics." *Northwest Journal of Teacher Education* 15:2 (2020) 1–11. https://doi.org/10.15760/nwjte.2020.15.2.6.

Stuessy, Carol, and Gilbert Naizer. "Reflection and Problem Solving: Integrating Methods of Teaching Mathematics and Science." *School Science and Mathematics* 96:4 (April 1996) 170–77.

Sugishita, Judy, and Rocio Dresser. "Social-Emotional Learning in a Field Course: Preservice Teachers Practice SEL-Supportive Instructional Strategies." *Journal of Inquiry & Action in Education* 10:1 (2019) 36–67.

Sutherland, Kevin S., and Nirbhay N. Singh. "Learned Helplessness and Students with Emotional or Behavioral Disorders: Deprivation in the Classroom." *Behavioral Disorders* 29:2 (February 2004) 169–81.

Tanguay, Carla Lynn, et al. "AAA+ Professional Development for Teacher Educators Who Prepare Culturally and Linguistically Responsive Teachers." *Curriculum and Teaching Dialogue* 20:1 (2018) 87–104.

Bibliography

Thompson, Phyllis I. "The Anatomy of a Teachable Moment: Implications for Teacher Educators." *Journal of Inquiry & Action in Education* 1:2 (2008) 19–34.

Tinker, Melvin. "Ministries of Mercy, Moral Distance and the Good Samaritan: The Challenge to Evangelical Social Action." *Churchman* 123 (Spring 2009) 53–65.

Tomlinson, Carol A. "One to Grow On: Respecting Students." *Educational Leadership* 69:1 (September 2011) 94–95.

Tough, Paul. *How Children Succeed: Grit, Curiosity, and the Hidden Power of Character.* Boston: Houghton Mifflin Harcourt, 2012.

Trna, Josef, et al. "Implementation of Inquiry-Based Science Education in Science Teacher Training." *Journal of Educational and Instructional Studies* 2:4 (2012) 199–209.

Unterhalter, Elaine. "What Is Equity in Education? Reflections from the Capability Approach." *Studies in Philosophy & Education* 28:5 (September 2009) 415–24. https://doi.org/10.1007/s11217-009-9125-7.

Van der Kolk, B. *The Body Keeps the Score: Brain, Mind, and Body in the Healing of Trauma.* New York: Viking, 2014.

Vigil, Patricia M., et al. "Developing Peacemakers in the Classroom: An Alternative Discourse in a Culture of War and Violence." *Peace Studies Journal* 6:1 (January 2013) 79–91.

Vygotsky, Lev S. *Mind in Society: The Development of Higher Psychological Processes.* Cambridge, MA: Harvard University Press, 1978.

Wagner, Maurice E. *The Sensation of Being Somebody: Building an Adequate Self-Concept.* Grand Rapids: Zondervan, 1975.

Walton, Gregory M. "The New Science of Wise Psychological Interventions." *Current Directions in Psychological Science* 23:1 (2014) 73–82.

Walvoord, John F. *Matthew: Thy Kingdom Come.* Chicago: Moody, 1974.

Warren, Michelle F. *The Power of Proximity.* Downers Grove, IL: InterVarsity, 2017.

Wenger, Etienne. *Community of Practice.* Cambridge: Cambridge University Press, 1998.

White, Frederick J. "Personhood: An Essential Characteristics of Human Species." *The Linacre Quarterly* 80:1 (February 2013) 74–97. https://doi.org/10.1179/002436391 2Z.0000000010.

Whitin, David J., and Phyllis Whitin. "Learning Is Born of Doubting: Cultivating a Skeptical Stance." *Language Arts* 76:2 (November 1998) 123–29.

Willis, Judy. "Teachable Moments Build Relational Memories." *Kappa Delta Pi* 43:3 (Spring 2007) 106–9.

Wilpow, Ray, et al. *The Heart of Learning and Teaching: Compassion, Resiliency and Academic Success.* Olympia, WA: Office of Superintendent of Public Instruction, 2016.

Windham, R. Craig, et al. "Selected Spiritual, Religious, and Family Factors in the Prevention of School Violence." *Counseling and Values* 49:3 (April 2005) 208–16.

Wolterstorff, Nicholas P. *Educating for Life: Reflections on Christian Teaching and Learning,* Grand Rapids: Baker Academic, 2002.

Wood, Leon J. *A Survey of Israel's History.* Grand Rapids: Zondervan, 1986.

Woodrow, Kelli. "Practicing Social Justice Education through Solidarity and Connection." *Curriculum and Teaching Dialogue* 20:1/2 (2018) 45–59.

Woolfolk Anita. *Educational Psychology.* 9th ed. Boston: Allyn and Bacon, 2004.

Wright, Jake. "The Truth, but Not Yet: Avoiding Naïve Skepticism via Explicit Communication of Metadisciplinary Aims." *Teaching in Higher Education* 29:3 (2019) 361–77. https://doi.org/10.1080/13562517.2018.1544552.

Wright, Travis. "Supporting Students Who Have Experienced Trauma." *NAMTA Journal* 42:2 (Spring 2017) 141–52.

Young, Iris M. *Social Justice and the Politics of Difference.* Princeton, NJ: Princeton University Press, 1991.

Yount, William R. *Created to Learn: A Christian Teacher's Introduction to Educational Psychology.* 2nd ed. Nashville: Broadman & Holman, 1996.

Zacarian, Debbie, et al. *Teaching to Strengths: Supporting Students Living with Trauma, Violence, and Chronic Stress.* Alexandra, VA: ASCD, 2017.

Zeichner, Kenneth M. *Educating Teachers for Cultural Diversity.* East Lansing, MI: National Center for Research on Teacher Learning, 1993.

Ziegler, Dave. "Optimum Learning Environments for Traumatized Children: How Abused Children Learn Best in School." n.d. http://poundpuplegacy.org/files/optimum_learning_environment.pdf.

Zimmerman, Barry J. "Attaining Self-Regulation: A Social Cognitive Perspective." In *Handbook of Self-Regulation*, edited by Monique Boekaerts, Paul R. Pintrich, and Moshe Zeidner, 13–39. San Diego: Academic, 2000.

Zohar, Danah, and Ian Marshall. *Spiritual Intelligence: The Ultimate Intelligence.* London: Bloomsbury, 2000.

Author Index

R

Reich, Robert, 103
Robertson, Douglas , 110, 111, 112

S

Safir, Shane, 158
Salend, Spencer, 69
Saphier, Jon, 123
Sapon-Shevin, Mara, 138
Schechter, Chen, 90, 91
Schreiner, Laurie, 2
Seamands, David, 55, 56
Seligman, Martin, 65, 107
Shanmugavelu, Genesan, 95, 97
Siegel, Harvey, 83
Souers, Kristin, 3, 4, 136
Stangor, Charles, 78, 84
Strong, Zoe, 131, 132
Sutherland, Kevin, 65

T

Thompson, Phillis, 77
Tinker, Melvin, 77
Tomlinson, carol, 95

U

Unterhalter, Elaine, 121

V

Van der Kolk, B. , 57–60
Vigil, Pat, 113, 116, 120
Vygotsky, Lev, 34

W

Warren, Michelle, 39
Wenger, Maurice, 106
White, Frederick, 24
Whitin, David, 93, 97–98
Willis, Judy, 137
Wilpow, Ray, 16, 145, 165
Wood, Leon, 75
Woodrow, Kelli, 124
Wright, Jake, 4, 91

Y

Young, Iris, 123
Yount, William, 86

Z

Zacarian, Debbie, 107
Zeichner, Ken, 80
Ziegler, Dave, 168
Zohar, Danah, 11

Subject Index